Peace

the POWER
of GOD'S PRESENCE

Book Three in the series
THE FRUIT OF THE SPIRIT:
THE PRODUCE OF GOD'S PRESENCE

Peace

the POWER *of* GOD'S PRESENCE

Book Three in the series
THE FRUIT OF THE SPIRIT:
THE PRODUCE OF GOD'S PRESENCE

by
SUSAN SLADE
and
SUSIE HALE

WS

WYATT & SONS
PUBLISHERS, LLC
Mobile, Alabama

Wyatt & Sons Publishers books may be ordered through booksellers or by contacting:

Wyatt & Sons Publishers, LLC
Mobile, Alabama 36695
www.wyattpublishing.com
editor@wyattpublishing.com

Because of the dynamic nature of the Internet, any web address or links contained in this book may have changed since publication and may no longer be valid.

Cover design by: Mark Wyatt
Interior design by: Mark Wyatt

ISBN 13:978-1-954798-36-6

Printed in the United States of America

DEDICATIONS

We dedicate this book first and foremost to our Prince of Peace, our Lord Jesus Christ, who has sustained us and continues to sustain us through some extremely difficult times.

I (Susan) dedicate this book to one of my spiritual dads, Precious Papa George Hearne, who constantly and consistently reminds me that I do not need to fret because our sovereign Father God is in control. Papa George is a servant of the Most High, an excellent listener who loves me with his whole heart; and God often uses him to calm me when I am upset or anxious.

I (Susie) dedicate this book to Mildred Garner who has become our "Auntie Mildred." She is a steadfastly calm person whom God uses to comfort, console, and encourage me. When the doctor informed me I would require major spine surgery, I was thankful Auntie Mildred was by my side! God used her to keep me steady in a moment that was truly overwhelming.

ACKNOWLEDGEMENTS

All of our Generous Gems—those who make regular donations to Precious Jewels Ministries, Inc. Without them, we would not be able to publish books.

Our PJM board members: Dane and Dana Carr, Crystal Foster, Eric Little, and Nick Miller who continue to encourage us, advise us, and pray for us.

Our Treasurer, Rick Ivey, who volunteers his time to help with the business end of running a non-profit corporation.

Our publisher, Mark Wyatt, and his wife Maryann for being encouragers and cheerleaders as we write, as well as publishing our books.

All of the prayer warriors that we can call, text, or email when we have a pressing need and know that we will be lifted before the Father.

Our precious friend and prayer partner, Melissa Blanchard, who wrote the Foreword.

Richard Albin, our photographer, who takes all our pictures and assists us with covers.

T. D. Hall (a.k.a. Coach) for encouraging us and sharing his wisdom.

SOLI DEO GLORIA!

The cover image is inspired by Revelation 4:3 (VOICE) "The One enthroned gleamed like jasper and carnelian, and a rainbow encircled the throne with an emerald glow."

FOREWORD

In our microwaveable society, we want things quickly, and we are often turned off at the thought of having to wait or do our part to get something, especially where God is concerned. I consider peace part of my birthright as a believer and never something I need to chase in the spirit realm. There have been times in my life where, if I were honest, I have chased the peace Jesus died to give me. After praying for many days regarding writing this for my chosen sister's book, I know that I can't truly understand peace as part of the "Fruit of the Spirit" without considering it from three critical perspectives.

First, we must consider peace from the perspective of peace with God. We cannot be at peace with God if we do not know Jesus as our Lord and Savior:

- Admit you are a sinner in need of Jesus as your Savior.
- Believe. Trust that Jesus died on the cross and rose again and that Jesus paid for your sins;
- Confess that Jesus is your Lord and Savior. Choose to let God be in charge of your life.

Salvation is the only way to achieve peace with God. Second, we can experience the peace of God. The trials of life have been enough to make me crave the peace of God. At the tender age of sixteen, my struggle with cerebral palsy caused me to contemplate committing suicide. I agree with what Ernest Hemingway wrote, "The world breaks everyone, and afterward, some are made strong in the broken places." Living in the peace of God is something I must learn to walk out as I go along. It has been vital for me to remember that God's peace cost Him: it is not cheap. Jesus died a cruel death on the cross to secure our peace with God and our ability to relax in the peace of God.

Finally, we must live in peace with others. Romans 12:18(NIV): "If possible, as it depends on you, live at peace with everyone." This scripture can challenge believers, but God can help us realize this truth daily. Sometimes, I can only live at peace with others when I agree to disagree on specific issues and keep moving. I suggest we pick our battles and remember that God's peace is better than anything a man can replicate. God's peace isn't like the peace the world offers.

If you are struggling to remain at peace, please get in touch with Precious Jewels Ministries and allow us to pray for you. This book was written with you in mind, and it would be our privilege to lift you in prayer. We also know that God's Word does not return void; therefore, we believe this book will bless countless people. We look forward to hearing how our readers were able to connect, be challenged, and maybe change as a result of this book.

Melissa Ann Blanchard
Author of Overcoming Mornings:
Jump Starting Your Day with God

Melissa and Susan Slade have been friends (really chosen sisters) for almost four-and-a-half decades since they met in their early teens at a school for disabled teenagers. At that time, they hoped and believed they would someday be in ministry together. God is faithful to complete what He has started and has now made what seemed impossible possible for them to work together through the wonder of modern technology even though they live hundreds of miles apart. Susie Hale has come to know Melissa through Facetime over the last several years and is now Melissa's chosen "Aunt Sue." We all look forward to the collaboration between the three of us in the future.

INTRODUCTION

*P*eace: *The Power of God's Presence* is the third book in the series, *The Fruit of the Spirit: The Produce of God's Presence*. We have fought hard to bring this book to you! It seems the more we studied peace, the more the enemy, Satan, tried to disturb ours. He tried to replace calm with chaos, but by the power of God's presence in our lives, he could not keep us down for long. A few examples of what God has brought us through while writing this book:

• Susan was literally "working blind" for much of our writing time due to cataracts in both eyes. Susie had to read everything aloud.

• Susan had cataract surgery on both eyes but discovered she also has glaucoma for which she must do eye drops twice daily.

• Susie had surgery to remove a ganglion cyst from the top of her foot that took much longer to heal than we had hoped.

• Susan's mother fell on her icy driveway and suffered compression fractures of three vertebrae: T1, T3, and T4.

•   Susan's mother went to the ER on March 25, 2025. She had a heart attack, severe anemia, and acute kidney injury resulting in kidney failure and requiring dialysis. She graduated to be with her Savior, Jesus, on June 13, 2025.

•   Many more personal situations have occurred, but Our Prince of Peace continues to prove Himself faithful.

Peace truly is a position of power enabled, activated, and actualized by the Holy Spirit within us! Throughout this book you will see Peace with God, the Peace of God, and the importance of Peace with Others. We pray you are empowered by God to live a life of shalom—nothing missing, nothing broken, complete wholeness!

Quotations are designated with numbers in parenthesis at the end of the quote and are listed on the "Notes" pages. Occasionally you will encounter an unusual word or phrase set off by quotation marks. You will find the definitions/explanations of those in the pages labeled "Susanisms". There is a section titled "Facets of Peace" listing the devotions under the categories of Peace with God, Peace of God, and Peace with Others as well as an Index of Scripture References in the back of the book. For those who may not have ever taken the first step to peace—Peace with God, there is a section titled "Jewels of Salvation" to help you become a part of the family of God followed by "Believer's Benefits."

Here are some suggestions on how to get the most out of this book:

• Read one devotional per day as your "daily quiet time" and reflect on it throughout the day.

• We call the last paragraph on each devotional the "challenge." Try to implement the suggestions, ask yourself hard questions, and ask the Holy Spirit to help you apply what you have learned.

• Many of the devotionals include a worship experience. Take the time to type the URL in your search engine and listen to or sing along with the suggested song. You may think of other hymns or spiritual songs that go with the theme of the day. Write those on the bottom of the page for future reference. If the song is word-for-word Scripture, try to memorize it!

• Insert your name or the name of a friend for whom you are interceding into Scripture. (i.e. Peace I leave with Susan; My peace I give to Susan; not as the world gives do I give to Susan. Do not let your heart be troubled, Susan, nor let it be fearful. John 14:27.)

• Here are a few of our favorite websites to help you with your own studies:

o www.biblegateway.com
Several versions of the Bible free and
study tools for a modest amount every
month.

o www.blueletterbible.com
Useful for finding the Strong's number
for specific words and many other free
helps.

o www.biblehub.com
Berean Standard Bible and other
translations. Useful cross references and
other tools.

o www.gotquestions.org
Answers to many biblical questions—
typical and obscure.

o https://webstersdictionary1828.com/
Great to look up words seldom used
today and often includes an example of
Scripture using the word.

QUOTES FROM OTHERS ON PEACE

"Joy is peace dancing. Peace is joy at rest."

Frederick Brotherton Meyer
https://www.goodreads.com/author/
quotes/6446816.F_B_Meyer

"If God be our God, He will give us peace in trouble. When there is a storm without, He will make peace within. The world can create trouble in peace, but God can create peace in trouble."

Thomas Watson, puritan preacher
https://christianquote.com/peace-in-trouble/

"No one can have the peace of God until they are at peace with God."

Jack Wellman
https://www.christianquotes.info/quotes-by-topic/
quotes-about-peace/

"To have peace, we must possess the Peace-Giver."

Billy Graham
https://billygraham.org/answer/three-kinds-of-peace-
what-the-bible-says/

"The world bases its peace on its resources, while God's peace depends on relationships. To be right with God means to enjoy the peace of God. The world depends on personal ability, but the Christian depends on spiritual adequacy in Christ. In the world, peace is something you hope for or work for, but to the Christian, peace is God's wonderful gift, received by faith. Unsaved people enjoy peace when there is an absence of trouble; Christians enjoy peace in spite of trials because of the presence of power, the Holy Spirit."

Warren Wiersbe

https://www.biblegateway.com/resources/wiersbe-be-bible-study/you-have-his-gift-peace-14-25-31

"The peace of God is a gift; it is not something we can manipulate because it is the fruit of oneness with Him. When our relationship with Him is strong and adversity strikes, we do not have to fall apart or give in to anxiety. We can choose to live in steadfast confidence of His love, wisdom, power, and provision. This is the basis of His unshakable peace—not that we are capable of controlling circumstances, but that His help is ever-present and perfect to deliver us in every challenge we face."

Charles F. Stanley

NASB Charles F. Stanley Life Principles Bible

"Peace should be a hallmark of the godly person."

Jerry Bridges in The Fruitful Life.

PEACE DEFINITIONS

Here we are listing the basic definitions of the words used for peace, peaceful, and peaceable in the Old and New Testaments. We have quoted these from *The Complete Word Study Dictionary: Old Testament* (1), Warren Baker and Eugene Carpenter, eds. and *The Complete Word Study Dictionary: New Testament*, Spiros Zodhiates, ed. (2) Each entry continues on to show the different nuances of the words in specific verses. These books are an excellent resource. The numbering system corresponds to *Strong's Exhaustive Concordance of the Bible.* (3)

HEBREW DEFINITIONS OF PEACE

H7965. šālôm: A masculine noun meaning peace or tranquility. This Hebrew term is used 237 times in the Old Testament and is used to greet someone (Judg. 19:20; 1 Chr. 12:18[19]; Dan. 10:19). It is common in Hebrew to ask how one's peace is (Gen. 43:27; Ex. 18:7; Judg. 18:15), which is equivalent to asking "How are you?" Moreover, this word was often used to describe someone's manner of coming or going; sometimes this took the form of a blessing: Go in peace (Judg. 8:9; 1 Sam. 1:17; Mal. 2:6). Another common expression involved dying or being buried in peace (Gen. 15:15; 2 Chr. 34:28; Jer. 34:5) Peace is present with the wise but absent from the wicked (Prov. 3:2, 17; Isa. 57:21; 59:8). It is often pictured as coming from God; Gideon built an altar and called the altar Yahweh-shalom (the Lord Is Peace; Num. 6:26; Judg. 6:24; Isa. 26:3).

H7999 *šālam*: A verb meaning to be safe, to be completed. The primary meaning is to be safe or uninjured in mind or body (Job 8:6; 9:4). This word is normally used when God is keeping His people safe. In its simple form, this verb also means to be completed or to be finished. This could refer to something concrete such as a building (1 Kgs. 7:51); or things more abstract, such as plans (Job 23:14). Other meanings of this verb include to be at peace with another person (Ps. 7:4[5]); to make a treaty of peace (Josh. 11:19; Job 5:23); to pay, to give a reward (Ps. 62:12[13]); to restore, repay, or make retribution (Ex. 21:36; Ps. 37:21).

GREEK DEFINITIONS OF PEACE

G1515. *eirḗnē*; gen. eirḗnēs, fem. noun. Peace.
(I) Particularly in a single sense, the opposite of war and dissension (Luke 14:32; Acts 12:20; Rev. 6:4). Among individuals, peace, harmony (Matt. 10:34; Luke 12:51; Acts 7:26; Rom. 14:19). In Heb. 7:2, "King of peace," means a peaceful king. Metaphorically peace of mind, tranquility, arising from reconciliation with God and a sense of a divine favor (Rom. 5:1; 15:13; Phil. 4:7 [cf. Is. 53:5]).

(II) By implication, a state of peace, tranquility (Luke 2:29; 11:21; John 16:33; Acts 9:31; 1 Cor. 14:33; 1 Thess.

5:3; Sept.: Judg. 6:23; Is. 14:30; Ezek. 38:8, 11).

(III) Peace, meaning health, welfare, prosperity, every kind of good. In Luke 1:79, "the way of peace" means the way of happiness; 2:14; 10:6, "son of peace" means son of happiness, i.e., one worthy of it; 19:42; Rom. 8:6; Eph. 6:15, "gospel of peace" means gospel of bliss, i.e., which leads to bliss; 2 Thess. 3:16. "The God of peace" means the author and giver of blessedness (Rom. 15:33; 16:20; Phil. 4:9; 1 Thess. 5:23; Heb. 13:20 [cf. Sept.: Is. 9:6, "the Prince of Peace"]). "Your peace" means the good or blessing which you have in Christ and share through salutation and benediction (Matt. 10:13; Luke 10:6; John 14:27). The expression "with peace" means with good wishes, benediction, kindness (Acts 15:33; Heb. 11:31). Simply "in peace" (1 Cor. 16:11; Sept.: Gen. 26:29; Ex. 18:23). As used in formulas of salutation, either at meeting or parting, see aspázomai (782), to embrace, to greet. Thus on meeting, the salutation is "Peace be unto you [eirḗnē humín]," meaning every good wish (Luke 24:36; John 20:19, 21, 26; Dan. 10:19). Also in letters (Rom. 1:7; 2:10; 1 Cor. 1:3; 2 Cor. 1:2; Gal. 1:3). In Luke 10:5, "Peace unto this house" (a.t.) means every good wish for this house; Sept.: Judg. 19:20; 1 Chr. 12:18. At parting, húpage (5217), go, meaning to go away in peace (Mark 5:34; James 2:16). The same with the verb poreúou from poreúomai (4198), to go in peace (Luke 7:50; 8:48; Acts 16:36; Sept.: Judg. 18:6; 1 Sam. 1:17; 20:42).

(IV) In the OT the equivalent word shalom (7965) meant wholeness, soundness, hence health, well–being, prosperity; more particularly, peace as opposed to war (Judg. 4:17; 1 Sam. 7:14; Eccl. 3:8 [cf. Luke 14:32; Acts 12:20; Rev. 6:4]), or concord as opposed to strife (Ps. 28:3; Jer. 9:8; Obad. 1:7 [cf. Matt. 10:34; 1 Cor. 7:15; Eph. 4:3 {see also Acts 24:2; 1 Thess. 5:3; Ps. 122:7; Is. 52:7; Jer. 29:7}]).

(V) God is said to be a God of peace, not as one who needs peace, but one who dispenses peace. He expects peace of His people, meaning the absence of confusion (Rom. 14:17; 1 Cor. 7:15; 14:33; Eph. 4:3; Heb. 12:14; Ps. 34:14; 35:20; Zech. 8:16). He rewards those who practice this peace (James 3:18 [cf. Matt. 5:9]), but those who disregard it are punished (Rom. 3:17 [cf. Is. 59:8, 9]). Peace is a blessing of which God alone is the author (Job 25:2; Ps. 147:14; Is. 45:7). He, being the author of peace, is the only one who can bestow it upon the righteous (Gen. 15:15, upon Abraham; 2 Kgs. 22:20, upon Josiah; Ps. 37:37, upon the perfect man; 119:165, upon those who love God's law; Prov. 3:2, upon those who follow divine wisdom [cf. James 3:18; Ps. 4:8; Job 5:23; Is. 32:17]). It is a gift which God desires to impart to all His people (Jer. 29:11), but which He is often unable to grant because of their sins (Sept.: Is. 48:18; Jer. 4:10 [cf. Jer. 4:14]). There can be no peace to the wicked (Sept.: Is. 57:19 [cf. Is. 57:20, 21; 48:22]). Those who hope for it, while continuing in their iniquity, are self–deceived (Sept.: Jer. 6:14; 8:15 [cf. Jer. 8:11; Ezek. 13:10, 16]).
(VI) Peace is the paramount blessing that Israel was looking for in the messianic kingdom (Num. 25:12;

Lev. 26:6; Is. 54:10; Ezek. 34:25; 37:26; Mal. 2:5, 6). The messenger who brings tidings of the coming salvation is one who publishes peace (Is. 52:7; Nah. 1:15). The Messiah Himself is the Prince of Peace (Is. 9:6 [cf. Mic. 5:5; Zech. 6:13]). Of the increase of His government and peace there shall be no end (Is. 9:7). See Ps. 29:11; 37:11; 72:3, 7, "In his days the righteous shall flourish; and abundance of peace so long as the moon endureth"; 122:7; Is. 54:13; 60:17; 66:12; Jer. 4:10; 6:14; 8:15; 14:13; 23:17; 28:9; 33:6; Hag. 2:9. The NT shares with the OT the view of peace as a characteristic of the messianic time (Luke 1:79; 2:14; 19:38; Acts 10:36). The identification of the coming of the Lord Jesus with the coming of the Messiah is often what the disciples meant with their greetings on their missionary journeys (Matt. 10:13; Luke 10:5, 6). In His farewell words to His disciples, Jesus names peace as a gift to them from Himself (John 14:27; 16:33, "My peace I give unto you . . . these things I have spoken unto you, that in me ye might have peace").

(VII) Characteristic of the NT is the view of peace as the present possession of the believer. In a single case it is used by Paul of that future blessedness which is to be expected by the righteous and the Parousía or Second Coming (Rom. 2:10), but in general it denotes the state of the Christian in this present life. It is so used by Jesus in His farewell promise, "My peace I give unto you" (John 14:27). It is thus represented by Paul (Rom. 5:1; 8:6; 15:13; 2 Thess. 3:16; Col. 3:15), in which case peace acquires the technical meaning of the tranquil state of a soul assured of its salvation through Christ, fearing nothing from God and consequently content with its earthly lot, whatever it is. This is the direct result of redemption by Christ (Eph. 2:15, 17) and consists primarily of a state of conscious reconciliation with God (Rom. 5:1), although it is often used in a broader sense to denote all the blessings which accompany and flow from that reconciliation (Rom. 1:7; 1 Cor. 1:3; 2 Thess. 3:16).

(VIII) Words with which eirénē are associated in the NT are as follows: agápē (26), love (2 Cor. 13:11; Eph. 6:23, "Peace . . . and love with faith"); cháris (5485), grace (Rom. 1:7; 1 Cor. 1:3; 2 Cor. 1:2; Gal. 1:3; Eph. 1:2; Phil. 1:2; Col. 1:2; 1 Thess. 1:1; 2 Thess. 1:2; 2 Tim. 1:2; 2 Tim. 1:2; Titus 1:4; Phile. 1:3; 1 Pet. 1:2; 2 Pet. 1:2; 2 John 1:3; Rev. 1:4); dóxa (1391), glory, and timḗ (5092), honor as the eschatological reward for working well (Rom. 2:10); dikaiosúnē (1343), righteousness; chará (5479), joy (Rom. 14:17); hope and joy (Rom. 15:13); peace and mercy (Gal. 6:16) aspháleia (803), safety, security, as the opposite of eschatological peril (1 Thess. 5:3). The NT concept of peace has nothing to do with the Stoic concept of apátheia (n.f.), indifference or apathy, and the Epicurean ataraxía (n.f.), selfish nondisturbance. The peace which God gives is never to be identified with selfish unconcern (cf. 1 Cor. 7:15; Phil. 4:7; Col. 3:15). God's peace is independent of outside conditions and is the fruit of an objective, real salvation with God.

G1516. *eirēnikós*; fem. eirēnikḗ, neut. eirēnikón, adj.

from eirḗnē (1515), peace. Pertaining to peace, peaceable or peaceful (Heb. 12:11, healthful, wholesome; James 3:17, peaceful, disposed to peace; Sept.: Deut. 2:26; Ps. 37:37; 120:7). The reference is to eirḗnē (1515), peace, as the blessing of salvation.

G1517. *eirēnopoiéō*; contracted eirēnopoiṓ, fut. eirēno-poiḗsō, from eirḗnē (1515), peace, and poiéō (4160), to make. To make peace, reconciliation (Col. 1:20; Sept.: Prov. 10:10). Eirēnopoiéō concerns itself with bringing about a cessation of hostilities while eirēneúō (1514) affects the attitudes of those concerned, to be at peace.

G1518. *eirēnopoiós*; gen. eirēnopoioú, masc. noun from eirēnopoiéō (1517), to make peace. Peacemaker. The one who, having received the peace of God in his own heart, brings peace to others (only in Matt. 5:9). He is not simply one who makes peace between two parties, but one who spreads the good news of the peace of God which he has experienced.

CONTENTS

Dedication   7

Acknowledgements   8

Foreword   10

Introduction   13

Quotes from Others About Peace   17

Peace Definitions   19

Genesis 15:13-16   God Grants Abram Peace   35

Genesis 26:26-31   Covenant of Peace Between Isaac
                        and Abimelech   38

Genesis 28:20-22   Jacob Promises Tithe to God 41

Genesis 37:4   Jealousy Disrupts Peace   44

Exodus 4:18   Go in Peace to Egypt   47

Exodus 18:23   Advice to Keep the Peace   49

Leviticus 26:6   The Blessing of Obedience is Peace 51

Numbers 6:26   Peace is a Present from God   54

Numbers 6:25-26   Our Father's Joy, Approval, and
                        Peace   56

Judges 6:22-24	Peace Through Submission to God's Plans	58
1 Samuel 20:42	Peace Pact Between Saul's Son and Anointed One	61
Psalm 4:8	Peaceful Sleep	64
Psalm 29:11	Blessed with Strength and Peace	66
Psalm 34:13-15	Passionately Pursue Peace	68
Psalm 37:11	Peace Prevails for the Meek Who Seek God's Kingdom	70
Psalm 72:7	Peace will Proliferate	72
Psalm 85:8-9	The Lord will Speak Peace	75
Psalm 119:165	Great Peace	78
Psalm 120:5-7	In Favor of Peace	81
Poem	Reaction to Terrorism of September 11, 2001	83
Psalm 122:6-8	Pray for the Peace of Jerusalem	84
Proverbs 3:1-6	Keeping Commandments Provides Peace	87

Proverbs 3:13-18	Peaceful Paths of Wisdom	91
Proverbs 12:20	Peace-Filled Joy	92
Proverbs 16:17	Enemies Live at Peace with Us	94
Isaiah 9:6	Sar Shalom Prince of Peace	97
Isaiah 9:7	Everlasting Kingdom of Peace	100
Isaiah 26:3-4	Kept in Perfect Peace	103
Isaiah 52:7	Beautiful Feet	105
Isaiah 53:5	Suffering Servant Brings Shalom	108
Isaiah 55:12	Led Forth in Peace	110
Matt 5:9	Peacemakers Look Like Papa	113
Mark 4:39	Peace, Be Still	115
Mark 5:33-34 and Lk 8:48	Go in Peace and Be Free	118
Mark 9:50	Peace Preservers	122
Luke 1:79	Prophet to Prepare the Way for the Prince of Peace	124

Luke 2:13-14	Peace on Earth	127
Luke 2:14	Christmas Poem by a Soldier's Mom	130
Luke 2:29-32	Shalom for Simeon	132
Luke 7:50	Faith Leads to Peace	136
Luke 19:38	Parade of the Prince of Peace	140
Luke 19:41-44	If Only You Had Known	143
Luke 24:35-43	Peace be with You	146
John 14:27	Legacy of Peace	149
John 16:32-33	Peace During Tribulation	151
John 20:19-21	Sent Out with Peace	155
John 20:26-29	Peace for the Doubter	158
Acts 9:31	Respite to Refuel and Refine	161
Acts 10:34-36	Peter Proclaims Gospel of Peace to the Gentiles	164
Romans 1:7	Grace and Peace to Believers in	

	Rome	168
Romans 2:9-11	The Peace of Christ is Inclusive, Not Exclusive	171
Romans 5:1	Through God's Grace, I Stand in Peace	176
Romans 8:5-10	The Mind of the Spirit is Life and Peace	179
Romans 12:17-21	Overcome Evil with Good	182
Romans 14:17-19	Pursue What Promotes Peace	185
Romans 15:13	Filled with Joy and Peace	189
Romans 15:33	God of Peace	192
Romans 16:20	God of Peace to Crush Satan	195
1 Cor. 1:3, 2 Cor. 1:2, Gal. 1:3, Eph.1:2, Phil. 1:2, 1 Thess. 1:1, 2 Thess. 1:2, Titus 1:4	Trending Now: Grace and Peace	198
2 Corinthians 13:11	Perfect Harmony: Live in Peace	200
Galatians 5:22	Fruit of the Spirit: Peace	203
Ephesians 2:13	I Will Testify About the Blood	205

Ephesians 2:11-18	Jesus: The Source of Peace for All Who Trust Him	207
Ephesians 4:1-3	Practice and Preserve the Bond of Peace	212
Ephesians 6:13-18	Boots of Peace?	216
Ephesians 6:23-24	Peace Progresses from God's Love	219
Phil 4:6-7, Psalm 138:3	Prevailing Peace	223
Philippians 4:8-9	Focus on Precious Perceptions	225
Colossians 1:2	Grace and Peace as a Greeting	228
Colossians 1:15-20	The Son Bled Peace into the World	231
Colossians 3:15-17	Let God's Peace Reign and Be Thankful	235
Colossians 3:15-17	May Your Peace Reign	237
1 Thessalonians 5:12-13	Live in Peace with Leaders	238
1 Thessalonians 5:23-24	God of Peace Himself	

	Sanctifies Us	241
2 Thessalonians 3:16	Peace Always in All Ways	245
1 Tim. 1:2, 2 Tim. :1-2	Grace, Mercy and Peace	248
2 Timothy 2:22	Hunt Down Harmony	251
Philemon 1:1-3	Grace and Peace to Philemon	253
Hebrews 12:9-11	Discipline Yields the Peaceful Fruit of Righteousness	256
Hebrews 12:14	Pursue Peace	259
Hebrews 13:20-21	May the God of Peace Equip You	262
James 3:17-18	Wisdom from Above	265
1 Peter 1:2b	Grace and Peace Be Yours in Abundance	268
1 Peter 3:8-11	Seek Peace and Pursue It	270
1 Peter 5:14	"Familyship"	274
2 Peter 1:2	Multiplication, Not Addition	276
2 Peter 3:14	Be Found at Peace Because Jesus Holds the Future	279

2 John 1:3   Greeting of Grace, Mercy,
                      and Peace   282

Jude 1:2   Multiplied Blessings   286

Summary Poem   Peace with God, the Peace of God,
                      and Peace with Others   289

Facets of Peace   291
Jewels of Salvation   296
Believers' Benefits   299
Dictionary of "Susanisms"   300
Index of Scripture References   303
Notes   310
Bibliography   325

GOD'S COVENANT WITH ABRAM

Then the LORD said to Abram, "Know for certain that your descendants will be strangers in a land that is not their own, and they will be enslaved and mistreated four hundred years. But I will judge the nation they serve as slaves, and afterward they will depart with many possessions. You, however, will go to your fathers in peace^{H7965} and be buried at a ripe old age. In the fourth generation your descendants will return here, for the iniquity of the Amorites is not yet complete. When the sun had set and darkness had fallen, behold, a smoking firepot and a flaming torch appeared and passed between the halves of the carcasses. On that day the LORD made a covenant with Abram, saying, "To your descendants I have given this land—from the river of Egypt to the great River Euphrates— the land of the Kenites, Kenizzites, Kadmonites, Hittites, Perizzites, Rephaites, Amorites, Canaanites, Girgashites, and Jebusites."

Genesis 15:13-21

In the first part of Genesis Chapter fifteen, God assured Abram (later to be renamed Abraham) that his heir would be his own biological son rather than his servant. God also promised Abram the land in which he was currently living. Abram asked how he would know this for certain. God had Abram cut certain animals in half and lay the two pieces side by side with a path between. This was part of a custom of "cutting covenant." The symbolism was that the two parties would walk between the pieces implying that this should be done to them if they broke the promise they were making to each other. Note that only God passed through the pieces, meaning that God is the one responsible for keeping His covenant with Abram to make him a great nation who possessed the Promised Land. The covenant relied on God's grace, not Abram's obedience.

In the middle of this covenant ceremony, God prophesied the four-hundred-year captivity of the nation of Israel in Egypt, but also assured Abram they would eventually return and possess the land. Where does peace come in? Abram believed what God promised and it was "credited to him as righteousness" (Genesis 15:6). God promised Abram he would enjoy a long life and die in peace. He could have the peace of God because by believing, by trusting God's promises, he had peace with God.

When we have a right relationship with God through trusting Jesus as our Lord and Savior, His peace is available to us. We can have "shalom." A good definition of "shalom" is "Nothing missing, nothing broken, completely whole." Are you feeling broken in any way today? Do you feel incomplete? First, be sure you have made peace with God by trusting Jesus and surrendering your will to His. Then, you can ask for the peace of God to replace all your anxiety and brokenness and make you complete in Christ.

Father, we thank You that we are granted peace with You because we have trusted Jesus who was sacrificed in our place on the cross. When we feel anxious, broken, or incomplete, please grant us Your peace, a calmness that cannot be shaken no matter what the circumstances.

Worship along with the Gaither Vocal Band singing "We are the Sands, We are the Stars": https://www.youtube.com/watch?v=G8Bs2o-3D-M&list=RDG8Bs2o-3D-M&start_radio=1

COVENANT OF PEACE
BETWEEN ISAAC
AND ABIMELECH

Later, Abimelech came to Isaac from Gerar, with Ahuzzath his adviser and Phicol the commander of his army. "Why have you come to me?" Isaac asked them. "You hated me and sent me away." "We can plainly see that the LORD has been with you," they replied. "We recommend that there should now be an oath between us and you. Let us make a covenant with you that you will not harm us, just as we have not harmed you but have done only good to you, sending you on your way in peace[H7695]. And now you are blessed by the LORD." So Isaac prepared a feast for them, and they ate and drank. And they got up early the next morning and swore an oath to each other. Then Isaac sent them on their way, and they left him in peace[H7695].

Genesis 26:26-31

Abimelech was the king of the Philistines. He had called out Abraham when he lied saying Sarah was his sister, not his wife (Genesis 20). In Genesis 26, Isaac did the same thing his father Abraham had done. He lied saying Rebekkah was his sister. However, Abimelech again discerned that this was not the truth. Isaac had moved into Philistine territory due to a drought and lived among them until the Lord blessed him so much that King Abimelech asked him to leave because he had become "too mighty" (Genesis 26:16). In the passage above, Abimelech seeks to form a treaty with Isaac.

> 26-31 Earlier Abimelech, acknowledging God's presence with Abraham (21:22), sought to enter into a covenant with him. Likewise, Abimelech acknowledged the Lord's presence with Isaac and sought to enter into a covenant with him. Isaac, like Abraham, was the source of blessing to those who sought him out. Isaac, like Abraham, trusted God and lived "in peace" with his neighbors. (4)

As his father, Abraham, had done before him, Isaac wisely agreed to enter into a covenant of peace with King Abimelech. He prepared a great feast as a part of cere-moniously celebrating their covenant together.

> Isaac and the leaders were able to reach an agreement. To seal the treaty, Isaac hosted a feast, for in that culture, to eat with others was to forge strong links of friendship and mutual sup-port. That same day, Isaac's servants found one of Abraham's wells (Gen. 21:25-31) and opened it, and Isaac gave it the original name, Beersheba. "The well of the oath" now referred to Isaac's treaty as well as Abraham's. (5)

When we have peace with God, we enjoy the peace of God—the unshakeable confidence of His care for us.

Having those first two aspects of peace enables us to have peace with other people. We will explore each of these facets of peace as we continue. In the back of this book will be an addendum categorizing each devotion as dealing with "Peace with God", the "Peace of God", or "Peace with Others."

Father, we pray that You will enable us to live at peace with others (Romans 12:18) as far as it depends on us. Help us recognize factors that could disrupt our peace with those around us and to deal with them according to Your will and ways.

JACOB PROMISES TITHE TO GOD

Then Jacob made a vow, saying, "If God will be with me and will keep me in this way that I go, and will give me bread to eat and clothing to wear, so that I come again to my father's house in peace[H7965], then the Lord shall be my God, and this stone, which I have set up for a pillar, shall be God's house. And of all that you give me I will give a full tenth to you."

Genesis 28:20-22 (ESV)

28:20 made a vow. Vows in the ancient world generally involved a request made of deity with a promise of a gift in return when the request is fulfilled. The request often concerned protection or provision, and the gift was typically a sacrifice or a donation to the sanctuary of the deity. The details in this chapter conform to that pattern. God has promised protection, provision and return to the land, so Jacob made those the condition of his proffered gift — a tithe ("a tenth," v. 22) of all that he acquires during his absence. (6)

In Genesis 28:10-15 Jacob stopped for the night on his journey to find a wife among his mother Rebekkah's people in Paddan Aram. In a dream, God reaffirmed that His covenant with Abraham and Isaac now passed on to Jacob. God promised Jacob descendants like the dust of the earth through whom all peoples would be blessed.

God affirmed that He would watch over Jacob and bring him back to his land. God promised His presence. Jacob believed God spoke to him, but his vow sounds a bit like he was not completely convinced that the Lord would see him through. His vow begins with IF God does all these things, THEN I will worship him by giving a tithe. "Peace" in this context means safety in coming and going, that he would return "in one piece" as *The Message Bible* puts it—unmolested and not missing anything.

From our perspective of having the entire Bible, we KNOW we can have this kind of peace.

Isaiah 26:3 *You will keep in perfect peace all who trust in you, all whose thoughts are fixed on you!*

Hebrews 12:2 *Let us fix our eyes on Jesus, the author and perfecter of our faith, who for the joy set before Him endured the cross, scorning its shame, and sat down at the right hand of the throne of God*

We can have peace for a literal journey or just as important, peace for each day as we ride planet earth. The key is to keep our thoughts on Jesus and trust in Him. How do we do this? We spend time daily in God's word and in prayer—keep the lines of communication with God open!

Father, we can come and go in peace knowing that You are with us every step of the way. No harm can come to us that is not filtered through Your love. Thank You for giving us peace even in the middle of trying circum-stances because You are our Prince of Peace!

JEALOUSY DISRUPTS PEACE

Now Israel loved Joseph more than any other of his sons, because he was the son of his old age. And he made him a robe of many colors. But when his brothers saw that their father loved him more than all his brothers, they hated him and could not speak peacefully[H7965] *to him.*

Genesis 37:3-4 (ESV)

37:3 tunic of many colors. The Septuagint (LXX) favored this translation of the Heb. phrase used by Moses, although some prefer "a long-sleeved robe" or "an ornamented tunic." It marked the owner as the one whom the father intended to be the future leader of the household, an honor normally given to the firstborn son. (7)

If we look back to Genesis 37:2, Joseph had "brought their father a bad report about" his older brothers. His brothers thought of him as a "tattle tale". On top of this, Jacob had recognized Joseph as the future leader of their tribe by giving him a special coat or tunic. The older brothers' jealousy developed into hatred and they "could not speak peacefully" to him or as some translations read "they did not have a kind word" for him. They were both hurt and angry, feeling their father had betrayed them by favoring their younger brother.

Many of us know the rest of Joseph's story. He had dreams that implied that he would rule over not just his brothers, but his father and mother as well, with the entire family bowing to him. This caused his brothers' envy to fester into absolute animosity toward him. We know they sold him into slavery but told their father he was killed by a wild beast. Ultimately, however, God used what they intended to harm him to elevate him to second in command of all Egypt! Even though his brothers, not recognizing him, bowed before him to beg for food during a drought, he eventually saved his entire family (and therefore, the nation of Israel) from famine by bringing them to Egypt. If you aren't familiar with the story of Joseph, read on through Genesis chapter 50 to see how God works all things together for our good in His own way and in His own timing (Romans 8:28).

Envy or jealousy in this story lead to hatred and unrest in Jacob's family. The peace that brothers should enjoy with each other was broken as the older brothers allowed jealousy to boil within them until it became hatred. God wants us to dwell in peace with others as much as it relies on us. If we feel envious of others, we need to confess it and ask the Lord to change our hearts. Christians are to be known by their love (John 13:35). We are to make every effort to be at peace with others (Romans 12:18).

Psalm 133:1 (VOICE) *How good and pleasant it is when brothers and sisters live together in peace!*

Is there someone in your life with whom you need to make peace? A biological sibling or a brother or sister in Christ? Do you need to forgive someone or ask their forgiveness? Are you envious of someone—a coworker, church member, neighbor or even a friend? Confess it and ask the Lord to replace that envy with His love, and like the song from Frozen™, "Let it go!" Do not let jealousy fester into animosity and steal your peace!

Father, being at peace with others is not always easy. Sometimes we are provoked but many times, if we are honest, we are just jealous. Help us to let go of attitudes that are not in keeping with Your commands. Help us to live at peace with everyone as much as possible through the power of Your Holy Spirt within us.

Listen to Josh F. Martin singing "What You Meant for Evil, God Meant for Good": https://www.youtube.com/watch?v=ZuJq7iMySW4&list=OLAK5uy_n0Pw-7NR-LOfcQHaysZuxvlX4Nbarcfy5Y

GO IN PEACE TO EGYPT

Then Moses went back to his father-in-law Jethro and said to him, "Please let me return to my brothers in Egypt to see if they are still alive." "Go in peace[H7965]," Jethro replied.

Exodus 4:18

A little history to preface this exchange between Moses, and his father-in-law, Jethro: God had appeared to Moses in the burning bush and commissioned him to deliver the Israelites from slavery in Egypt. God had given Moses several proofs or "signs" to convince Moses that He was God, and Moses was the one God wanted to send on this mission. Once Moses was certain that God would speak through him and allow him the help of his brother, Aaron, he left the place of his encounter with God and went to Midian to talk to Jethro. Jethro was not only his father-in-law but was also his employer. Even though He was certain of his calling from God, he still extended the courtesy of giving his boss notice that he was leaving and asking his father-in-law for permission.

4:18 Please let me go. Courtesy toward the father-in-law for which he worked was not overlooked because of the divine call to service as national leader. Exactly how much was explained of the encounter at the burning bush remains unknown, but the purpose for the return, "and

47

see whether they are still alive," suggests that specific details of the call for him to be leader/deliverer were left unsaid, in contrast to the full explanation given to Aaron (v. 28). (8)

18 Moses left the region of Sinai and went to Midian to ask Jethro's permission to return to Egypt. Even the call of God did not erase the need for human courtesy and respect. (9)

By saying "Go in peace," Jethro was giving his blessing on Moses' journey. To go in "shalom" indicated that there would be no ill feelings between them as well as his hope that the journey would be peaceful—that God would protect and provide for Moses.

What can we apply to our lives from this story? We want to be at peace with others, including those for whom we work. We should strive not to "burn bridges" if we choose to leave a job for other employment, i.e. give required notice and try to part with good relationships intact. We should show proper respect to our elders as Moses did with his father-in-law. We are able to do this because we are at peace with God and enjoy the peace of God. Having peace within makes it easier to live in peace with others.

Father, help us to live in peace with others, to leave a situation peacefully, to show respect to whom it is due in order to be at peace.

ADVICE TO KEEP THE PEACE

If you follow this advice and God so directs you, then you will be able to endure, and all these people can go home in peace.[H7965]

Exodus 18:23

If you do what I advise and God directs you, then you will be able to handle the pressure. Not only that, but all these people standing around needing help, they will be able to return to their tents at peace.

Exodus 18:23 (VOICE)

What advice had Jethro given Moses? When Jethro brought his daughter Zipporah and grandsons to their father, Moses, in the wilderness he was concerned about the way Moses was handling disputes among the Israelites. Moses was trying to do it all himself, but he was just one man trying to govern at least two million people! Yikes!!! Jethro cautioned him against burning out and proposed a flow chart for delegating this responsibility. He instructed Moses to choose from the people wise, godly men of character, who would not be tempted to take bribes, to judge the lesser disputes among all the people. Only the most important cases would be brought before Moses. In this way, the people would still remain at peace with each other, and Moses would not be physically, spiritually, and emotionally taxed beyond human limits.

Exodus 18:14–23 Jethro knew that Moses' leadership was crucial for the future success of Israel and that any activity that drained his energy or wasted his time was bound to hurt the nation. Also, he didn't want his son-in-law to wear himself out and leave Zipporah a widow and his two grandsons without a father. No one man could minister personally to two million people and last very long. Moses had to confess that the work was too much for him (Num. 11:14). (10)

Jesus taught us "Blessed are the peacemakers, for they will be called sons of God" (Matthew 5:9). We, like Moses, need to realize that many times we cannot be the peacemaker alone. We must rely on the Holy Spirit within us, but we must also have the wisdom to seek godly advice and help when the task becomes overwhelming. Where do we need to be peacemakers? In our homes, with our extended families, in our schools, in our churches, in our workplaces, and sometimes in our communities—wherever God has planted us. If God sends us a "Jethro" to advise us not to try to do everything ourselves, we need to listen.

Father, help us to be peacemakers in our sphere of influence. Help us to work with others to achieve peace. May Your peace flow through us. May we be living examples of shalom—nothing missing, nothing broken, completely whole!

THE BLESSING OF OBEDIENCE IS TO LIVE IN PEACE

If you follow My statutes and carefully keep My commandments, I will give you rains in their season, and the land will yield its produce, and the trees of the field will bear their fruit. Your threshing will continue until the grape harvest, and the grape harvest will continue until sowing time; you will have your fill of food to eat and will dwell securely in your land. And I will give peace[H7965] to the land, and you will lie down with nothing to fear. I will rid the land of dangerous animals, and no sword will pass through your land. You will pursue your enemies, and they will fall by the sword before you. Five of you will pursue a hundred, and a hundred of you will pursue ten thousand, and your enemies will fall by the sword before you. I will turn toward you and make you fruitful and multiply you, and I will establish My covenant with you.

Leviticus 26:3-9

26:3–46 These blessings and curses conclude the treaty between God (as the superior party) and Israel recorded in Exodus – Leviticus (cf. Dt 27 – 28). In the ancient Near East, blessings and curses could be appended to a law collection in order to encourage obedience. (11)

God gave the Israelites an if/then sentence. If they are obedient—"follow My statutes and carefully keep My commandments"—then they will have peace in their land. God specifies what that looks like in the remaining verses. Then God lays out the consequences—curses—of disobedience. We know from reading the rest of the Old Testament and from the study of history that the Israelites failed to be obedient, and God allowed their enemies to take them away to captivity. At the end of Leviticus 26, however, God gives them the hope of being restored to their land and to right relationship with him if they repent—turn around from idol worship and the resulting wickedness—to worship and follow Him alone.

We, too, will have peace with God and the peace of God in our lives as we are obedient to His commands. We are saved by grace through faith in Jesus Christ, by believing He was the Son of God who died in our place on the cross and was raised to life on the third day and now reigns with the Father in Heaven. However, our inner peace can be disrupted while we reside on planet earth. Many times, that disruption comes from our refusing to walk in the will and ways of our Lord. Just like the Israelites, when we repent—turn from disobedient and destructive ways—and turn back to obeying our Father who loves us more than anyone else can, He will restore our peace. If you are not at peace today, make sure you are at peace with God by surrendering your life to Him. If you know you have that relationship with Him, sincerely pray asking Him to show you anything you need to change in order for the peace of God to reign in your life.

Father, we thank You that inner peace is available to us when we walk according to Your will and ways and keep our eyes fixed on Jesus (Hebrews 12:2).

PEACE IS A PRESENT FROM GOD

Then the LORD said to Moses, "Tell Aaron and his sons: This is how you are to bless the Israelites. Say to them: 'May the LORD bless you and keep you; may the LORD cause His face to shine[H215] *upon you and be gracious to you; may the LORD lift up His countenance toward you and give you peace*[H7965]*.' So they shall put My name on the Israelites, and I will bless them."*

Numbers 6:22-27

H215: 1) to be or become light, shine 1a) (Qal) 1a1) to become light (day) 1a2) to shine (of the sun) 1a3) to become bright 1b) (Niphal) 1b1) to be illuminated 1b2) to become lighted up 1c) (Hiphil) 1c1) to give light, shine (of sun, moon, and stars) 1c2) to illumine, light up, cause to shine, shine 1c3) to kindle, light (candle, wood) 1c4) lighten (of the eyes, his law, etc) 1c5) to make shine (of the face). (12)

When a new father is handed his baby for the first time, his eyes light up; and he may even have the sparkle of tears of joy in his eyes. Our heavenly Father's face lights up and shines down on us in grace and peace. The peace God gives us is not the temporary absence of any kind of trouble or trial. He grants us the ability to remain at peace, having a sense of wellness and wholeness even when the storm rages around us.

In some churches the pastor pronounces this blessing over the congregation as a benediction or parting statement. We know of more than one church choir that sings some version of this passage to end their service each week. This is the benediction the Lord instructed Moses to have Aaron and his sons pronounce over the Israelites, God's chosen people. We, too, are His chosen, adopted children; and this blessing is ours as well.

We would do well to memorize this blessing. Singing one of the many settings of it would help you to internalize these words. Meditate on the fact that God "keeps" you—protects and provides. He beams when you come before Him in prayer. He graciously saved you and holds you in His hands. He gives you His peace that "surpasses all comprehension" (Philippians 2:7) when you trust in Him.

Father, thank you for protecting, providing, and giving us peace no matter what trials we may face. Thank You for blessing us, Your children.

Worship along with churches across the United Kingdom:
https://www.youtube.com/watch?v=PUtll3mNj5U

Or enjoy a more traditional setting of this passage here:
https://www.youtube.com/watch?v=Nxn6tmVSljU

May the Lord bless and protect you; may the Lord's face radiate with joy because of you; may he be gracious to you, show you his favor, and give you his peace.

Numbers 6:25-26 (TLB)

The Lord make His face shine upon you [with favor], And be gracious to you [surrounding you with loving-kindness]; The Lord lift up His countenance (face) upon you [with divine approval], And give you peace [a tranquil heart and life].

Numbers 6:25-26 (AMP)

OUR FATHER'S JOY, APPROVAL, AND PEACE

My earthly father would come home from the night shift,
empty the change from his pockets and smile down at me.
The pennies, nickels, and dimes were not my only gift,
For his presence was more valuable than the presents,
you see.

I was at peace when my Daddy was near me,
no fear of harm because I trusted in his care.
I enjoyed confidence to play boldly and freely
as long as my strong, loving Daddy was there.

My Heavenly Father approvingly smiles down on me, too.
Father's face radiates joy, and He showers me with presents.
I am at peace because Father God gives grace each day anew.
God calls me His treasure and blesses me with His presence.

I know my Father will always be near me.
I need not fear as I cast upon Him all my cares.
I can live confidently, boldly, and freely
because my strong, loving Father will always be there.

Worship opportunity: Imagine God the Father singing this song to you as His child and as the Bride of Christ as you listen to Steven Curtis Chapman singing the song he wrote for his wife, Mary Beth, called "I Will Be Here": https://www.youtube.com/watch?v=vU2hPIwqbTk

PEACE THROUGH SUBMISSION TO GOD'S PLANS

When Gideon realized that He was the Angel of the LORD, he said, "Oh no, Lord GOD! I have seen the Angel of the LORD face to face!" But the LORD said to him, "Peace^H7965 to you. Don't be afraid, for you will not die." So Gideon built an altar to the LORD there and called it Yahweh Shalom^H7965. It is in Ophrah of the Abiezrites until today.

Judges 6:22-24

6:22-23 Likely in verse 22 Gideon had in mind the Lord's words to Moses, "You cannot see my face, for humans cannot see me and live" (Exod 33:20). But in response to Gideon's fear, the Lord assured him that he would live (Judg 6:23). It's clear, then, that Gideon did not see the full, unshielded expression of God's glory. (13)

Most likely what Gideon experienced was a "theophany", a clear manifestation of God in visible form. Many times, "Angel of the Lord" refers to the pre-incarnate Christ appearing to a human—a "Christophany"—which would be consistent with Gideon not being in danger from looking upon Him. When Jesus walked on earth, He did not reveal His glorified state, nor did He when He appeared to Gideon. Gideon clearly realized that God Himself was speaking to him and was rightly fearful. However, God the Son, Jesus, assured Gideon he would not die and instead gave him the greeting of "Peace", shalom.

> 6:24 The Hebrew word for "peace" (shalom) means much more than a cessation of hostilities: It carries with it the ideas of well-being, health, and prosperity. Gideon now believed the Lord was able to use him, not because of who he was, but because God is a God of provision and peace. We can pray for that same kind of contented purposefulness in our relationship with God. (14)

Shalom encompasses total well-being, the peace of God. What does Warren Wiersbe mean by "contented purposefulness"? When we realize we are "called according to God's purposes" (Romans 8:28), and we submit our lives to be conformed to the image of Christ (Romans 8:29), we will be "content".

> CONTENT, *adjective* [Latin , to be held; to hold.] Literally, held, contained within limits; hence, quiet; not disturbed; having a mind at peace; easy; satisfied, so as not to repine, object, or oppose. (15)

We are most content or peaceful when we are in obedience to the Lord, bringing pleasure and glory to His name. Paul wrote to Timothy:

1 Timothy 6:6 *Of course, godliness with contentment is great gain.*

Are you experiencing a feeling of discontentment or a lack of peace? We only have the peace of God when we have peace with God. Ask the Lord to reveal any area where you may not be wholeheartedly, completely following Jesus. Then make any necessary changes to draw nearer to God by obedience to His word—safely contained within the limits, the boundaries God sets. The enablement to do this is a result of the Holy Spirit's power within you as a believer.

Father, help us to remain within the boundaries You have set before us in Your word in order to be at peace and free to live the abundant life You offer us.

PEACE PACT BETWEEN SAUL'S SON AND ANOINTED ONE

At last Jonathan said to David, "Go in peace[H7965], for we have sworn loyalty to each other in the Lord's name. The Lord is the witness of a bond between us and our children forever." Then David left, and Jonathan returned to the town.

1 Samuel 20:42 (NLT)

We need a little background to understand the magnitude of this peace agreement. Jonathan was the eldest son of Saul, the first king of Israel, and heir apparent to the throne. However, we read in 1 Samuel 15 that Saul disobeyed God's instruction to completely annihilate the Amalekites and even their cattle. Therefore, the Lord chose not to continue the kingship through Saul's heirs.

1 Samuel 15:26b & 28 *"For you have rejected the word of the Lord, and the Lord has rejected you from being king over Israel" . . . And Samuel said to him, "The Lord has torn the kingdom of Israel from you this day and has given it to a neighbor of yours, who is better than you."*

In 1 Samuel 16, the Lord has Samuel anoint David as the next king, but David does not take the throne immediately. In Chapter 17, we have the famous confrontation between Israel and the Philistines in which David slays the Philistine champion, a nine- foot tall "giant" named Goliath. Saul's son, Jonathan, and David who would take his place as the future king were drawn together by God.

1 Samuel 18:1 (AMPC) *When David had finished speaking to Saul, the soul of Jonathan was knit with the soul of David, and Jonathan loved him as his own life.*

Jonathan went on to make a covenant with David in which he gave David his own robe, armor, sword, bow, and belt. In essence, he was dressing David like a prince, an heir to the throne.

In the current passage, Saul has determined to kill David, but Jonathan warns him of Saul's anger. When Jonathan tells David to "go in peace," he is giving his blessing on David as the future king. They have renewed their covenant to stand for each other and that one would take care of the children of the other if anything happened to one of them. This bond, this covenant of peace, was to last between their heirs forever. In 2nd Samuel, we read that David remembered this vow of friendship and found that Jonathan had a surviving son named Mephibosheth who was lame in both legs. Most kings of that era would kill all heirs of the previous king. Instead, David took Mephibosheth under his wing in peace, had him eat at the king's table, and returned to Mephibosheth all that had belonged to Saul and his household. He commanded Saul's servants to work the land to give Mephibosheth his own means of support, giving him standing and dignity.

Peace (*shalom*) with others is not just an absence of conflict. It is truly desiring each other's wellbeing and wholeness. We can only have this kind of peace with our brothers and sisters in Christ when we already have peace with God and the peace of God. Then the Holy Spirit enables God's peace to flow through us and into our relationships. If there is conflict between you and another member of God's family, ask the Holy Spirit to replace chaos and conflict with calmness and the ability to seek peace. Pray for the other person's peace (wellness and wholeness) and allow the Lord to replace any animosity with true brotherly/sisterly love.

Father, the Lord Jesus said, "God blesses those who work for peace, for they will be called the children of God" (Matthew 5:9 NLT). May Your Holy Spirit enable us to seek peace with others.

PEACEFUL SLEEP

I will lie down and sleep in peace[H7965], for You alone, O LORD, make me dwell in safety.

Psalm 4:8

In the first few verses of Psalm 4, David is praying about the fact that his enemies not only engage in combat, but they also attack him by maligning his character, lying about him. He asks how long this is going to continue. However, as he turns to the Lord, he is reminded that God is good and is able to protect him, physically, emotionally, and spiritually.

> Reassured of the Lord's all-sufficiency, the psalmist's inner agitation subsides. He can now lie down in peace and sleep, knowing that it is the LORD who makes him dwell in safety. What a change prayer has produced in only eight short verses! (16)

> Peace with God is the fruit of oneness with God. Ps. 4:8 (17)

David's attitude has been transformed as he communed with his Lord. He was assured of God's ability to protect him from his enemies. However, the peace in which he sleeps is not just the cessation of military attacks. It is the internal peace, the overall confidence of wellbeing. His mind can rest peacefully because God has made him whole. He has the peace of God that reassures him and silences any anxiety as he prays and submits his situation to the Lord.

There are times in our lives when we feel restless, anxious, or even fearful. We may be in a dangerous situation or be facing a troubling diagnosis. Like David, there may be people in our lives making false accusations against us. Our best resource is always prayer because when we honestly seek the Lord, when we enter into communion with Him, He can calm our hearts and allow us to sleep peacefully. Having trouble going to sleep? Pray until the Lord allows you to rest in His perfect peace despite ongoing trials. The peace of God does not depend upon a change of circumstances. His peace defies human logic by allowing us to be calm even while the storms of life rage, swirling around us. God's peace is available in all ways, always.

Father, thank You that You can give us peace that surpasses human understanding (Philippians 4:6-7). Help us to always turn to You during difficult times.

Memorize this scripture by singing along with "I Will Lie Down and Sleep-Psalm 4:8" from the album "Bible Memory Melodies" by Steve Green: https://www.youtube.com/watch?v=cqaY9H2N2jk&list=RDcqaY9H2N-2jk&start_radio=1

BLESSED WITH STRENGTH AND PEACE

The LORD gives His people strength; the LORD blesses His people with peace[H7965].

Psalm 29:11

The earlier verses of this psalm depict the majestic, mighty power of God. He controls the universe with His voice. In fact, He created the earth by speaking it into existence. He controls the wind, the rain, the lightening. A storm is a demonstration of His omnipotence—He is all-powerful.

> The power of God in a storm is great, and it is He who gives strength during a storm. God can strengthen and enable us to go through the storms of life and know what peace is afterward. The storm with all of its fury may lash across the land, but Jehovah is still in control. In every storm of life He is in control, and He will bless His people with peace. (18)

God demonstrates His power in literal storms, but we must remember He controls the storms of life as well. More importantly, His presence in our life determines our reaction to those storms. Are we panicking or peaceful? When we turn to the Lord and fix our minds on Him, we are blessed with His peace. How can we move from panic to peace? Prayer and soaking in Scripture that reminds us of His tender care for us such as:

John 10:11a *I am the good shepherd.*

Psalm 23:1 *The LORD is my shepherd; I shall not want.*

1 Peter 5:7 *Cast all your anxiety on Him, because He cares for you.*

We have a choice each time we face a trial. Will we panic and be paralyzed by anxiety, or will we saturate our minds with God's Word and prayer until the blessing of His peace saturates us?

Father, Susan and I have faced many storms, physical challenges together, some so drastic I nearly gave in to panic. However, You blessed me with Your peace as I placed all my anxiety upon You. Thank You for reminding me of Your loving care.

Worship with Casting Crowns as they sing, "Praise You in This Storm":
https://www.youtube.com/watch?v=0YUGwUgBvTU

PASSIONATELY PURSUE PEACE

Who is the man who delights in life, who desires to see good days? Keep your tongue from evil and your lips from deceitful speech. Turn away from evil and do good; seek^{H1245} peace^{H7965} and pursue^{H7291} it.

Psalm 34:13-15

King David is giving his subjects wise counsel and instruction on how God's people should behave. Our attitudes and actions should reflect God's mercy, justice, and love (Micah 6:8) If a person wants to have an enjoyable life, they should obey the Lord. They should watch their words, speak truthfully and kindly. They should walk away from any type of wrongdoing, and purposefully choose to do the right thing. They should seek peace first with God who will give them His peace within. Then they can strive for peace with other people. Peace is not always easy to achieve, but we should actively pursue–run and hunt down—peace. This passage is not just talking about peace with other nations, but peace in all relationships.

> H1245.... bâqash, baw-kash'; a primitive root; to search out (by any method, specifically in worship or prayer); by implication, to strive after:— ask, beg, beseech, desire, enquire, get, make inquisition, procure, (make) request, require, seek (for). (19)

H7291 râdaph, raw-daf'; a primitive root; to run after (usually with hostile intent; figuratively [of time] gone by):—chase, put to flight, follow (after, on), hunt, (be under) persecute(-ion, -or), pursue(-r). (20)

Is there a circumstance that is disturbing your peace within? Pray asking the Prince of Peace to give you His peace in the situation. Are you at odds with someone? Are you holding a grudge against someone or is someone not happy with you? Pray asking the Lord to help you restore peace in that relationship. Go to that person with the offer of peace. Paul urges us in Romans 12:18 (NIV), "If it is possible, as far as it depends on you, live at peace with everyone."

Father, thank You for sending Jesus to die on the cross and pay the penalty for our sin in order to restore our peace with You. Help us to actively pursue peace with others.

PEACE PREVAILS FOR THE MEEK WHO SEEK GOD'S KINGDOM

But the meek shall inherit the earth; and shall delight themselves in the abundance of peace[H7965].

Consider the blameless and observe the upright, for posterity awaits the man of peace[H7965]. But the transgressors will all be destroyed; the future of the wicked will be cut off.

Psalm 37:11, 37-38

The meek are those who are humbly committed and submitted to God, whose desire is to further the Lord's kingdom and agenda rather than their own. On a video, Bill Gaither shared this great definition: "Meekness is strength under control." The meek are those who wait patiently for the Lord. Patience is forged in trials and adversities. According to Psalm 37, the evildoers often appear to prosper in this world; but in God's economy their prosperity is only for a short while. God laughs at their haughtiness because He knows their end will be that of destitution, devoid of all that is good, apart from His presence forever. But the humble servants of God inherit the earth. What does this mean? Does it only mean the peaceful New Earth of eternity, or is there some provision for us now? We will inherit a peaceful New Earth at the end of the age when God casts Satan and all those who reject Jesus into the abyss of eternal punishment.

However, in this present life, believers have the "peace of God which surpasses all understanding" (Philippians 4:7), despite difficult circumstances. How do we experience that peace in the middle of our storms? We seek intimate relationship with our sovereign Lord who has the power over all circumstances through His word and prayer. Our "coach", T.D. Hall says, "The bigger God is in our lives, the smaller our problems are." We humbly make the needs and desires of our hearts known to our Heavenly Father, thanking Him in advance that He will be and provide everything we need. Because we as believers have the relationship of being God's children, His desire is to provide all that we need, all that is for our best. Those who reside in God's peace and at peace with others will have a posterity, a future. We can stand on that hope.

Father, help us to internalize the following verses of Scripture to be reminded that Your peace can reign in our lives here and now: Philippians 4:6-7, 1 Peter 5:7, Matthew 6:33, Romans 8:16-18, Romans 14:17.

PEACE WILL PROLIFERATE

May the righteous flourish in his days and prosperity^{H7965} abound, until the moon is no more.

Psalm 72:7 (BSB)

In his days may the righteous flourish, and peace^{H7965} abound, till the moon be no more!

Psalm 72:7 (ESV)

This Psalm is sometimes credited to Solomon. However, it seems to be a blessing David prayed over Solomon when he became king since verse 20 states "The prayers of David, the son of Jesse, are ended". It is a blessing for long life, prosperity, and a peaceful reign.

72:1–20 This is a Coronation Psalm, dedicated to the prosperity of Solomon at the beginning of his reign (1 Kin. 2). No NT writer applies any of the psalm to Christ. Still, since the Davidic kings and the Messiah's rule occasionally merge into each other in the OT literature, the messianic inferences here ought not to be missed (vv. 7, 17; cf. Is. 11:1–5; 60–62). This psalm describes a reign when God, the king, nature, all classes of society, and foreign nations all live together in harmony. (21)

72:7 He will be the true Melchizedek—King of righteousness and King of peace. During His reign justice will flourish, and peace will abound, until the moon ceases to exist. Notice that righteousness precedes peace. "The work of righteousness will be peace, and the effect of righteousness, quietness and assurance forever" (Isa. 32:17). By His righteous work for us on the cross, He bequeathed peace to us. And by His righteous rule He will one day bring peace to the war-torn world. (22)

Solomon's reign was characterized by righteousness, justice and peace. He began well by asking the Lord for wisdom (1 Kings 3:5-12). He was remembered as a wise leader. He championed the poor until the latter part of his reign. Solomon eventually made some poor choices despite his wisdom. He had multiple wives and concubines, many of whom did not worship the one, true God (1 Kings 11:1-3). Therefore, idolatry was common in Israel and in Solomon's own household. Although Solomon enjoyed a peaceful reign for the most part, peace did not abound "until the moon was no more." Therefore, we believe this Psalm may also be foreshadowing the reign of the Messiah, Jesus, our King of kings, and Lord of lords.

Jesus is the "Prince of Peace" in every way. He enables all three facets of peace in our lives. By His death on the cross and subsequent resurrection, He opened the pathway to our peace with God, paying the price to satisfy God's wrath against sin. When we trust in Jesus as Lord and Savior, His Holy Spirit comes to dwell in us and give us the peace of God that surpasses all understanding (Philippians 4:6-7). That same Holy Spirit enables us to have peace with others as we apply God's word to our relationships. Peace is one of the Fruit of the Spirit listed in Galatians 5:22-23 which can only be effective in our lives when Christ lives in and through us.

We look forward to and long for the day that Jesus will reign on the earth. However, we are to pray for and in every way possible to live "peaceful and quiet lives" here and now. Perhaps we all need to make this our daily prayer:

1 Timothy 2:1-4 (BSB) *First of all, then, I urge that petitions, prayers, intercessions, and thanksgiving be offered for everyone— for kings and all those in authority—so that we may lead tranquil and quiet lives in all godliness and dignity. This is good and pleasing in the sight of God our Savior, who wants everyone to be saved and to come to the knowledge of the truth.*

Father, we lift up our leaders to You, both local and national, that You would give them the wisdom to seek peace. We thank You that You are our true, all-wise, ever-present King and can turn the hearts of our earthly leaders as easily as You change the course of a stream.

Proverbs 21:1 (NLT) *The king's heart is like a stream of water directed by the LORD; he guides it wherever he pleases.*

THE LORD WILL SPEAK PEACE

I will listen[H8085] to what God the LORD will say[H1696]; for He will surely speak[H1696] peace[H7965] to His people and His saints; He will not let them return to folly[H3690]. Surely His salvation is near to those who fear Him, that His glory may dwell in our land.

Psalm 85:8-9

H3690. kislāh: A feminine noun meaning foolishness, stupidity, confidence. The root idea of fatness (see kāsal[3688]) may have two implications. In Job 4:6, kesilāh means the confidence of one who is fat and firm. Eliphaz cast doubt on Job's righteousness by asking why he was confused if he really feared God. In Psalm 85:8[9], on the other hand, God warned His restored people not to return to their former folly. In that verse, the word refers to sluggish foolishness that is no longer alive to the fear of God. (23)

In the context of verse 8, the Hebrew word for "say" and "speak" could mean to declare as in "I will listen to what God the Lord will declare, for He will surely declare peace . . ." The word translated "listen" often means to "hear intelligently often with implication of attention, obedience . . ." (Strong's H8085). When we are listening attentively to what the Lord declares (in our case reading it in His word) and trusting Jesus for our salvation, we will have peace with God and the peace of

God. In addition, the Holy Spirit within us will prevent us from straying from God's path and venturing back into the old ways of placing our confidence in our own works, the folly of trusting self rather than Jesus. We must realize our dependence on His dying on the cross in our place and glorious resurrection. The Apostle Paul warns in Philippians 3 against placing confidence in the works of the flesh:

Philippians 3:2-3 (BSB) *Watch out for those dogs, those workers of evil, those mutilators of the flesh! For it is we who are the circumcision, we who worship by the Spirit of God, who glory in Christ Jesus, and who put no confidence in the flesh . . .*

Philippians 3:2-3 (VOICE) *Watch out for the dogs—wicked workers who run in packs looking for someone to maul with their false circumcision. We are the true circumcision—those who worship God in Spirit and make our boast in Jesus the Anointed, the Liberating King—so we do not rely on what we have accomplished in the flesh . . .*

Paul then proceeds to list all of his accomplishments which would far surpass most of his listeners but concludes in Philippians 3:8 that all his "righteous works" done apart from Christ are "rubbish," "garbage," or in some translations, "dung."

Since the Lord has shown us extreme mercy and grace by sending His Son to die in our place, the response to such great love should be a desire to please Him by obeying Him. We cannot obey what God has declared unless we know what that is. In our case, reading the Bible as the Holy Spirit within us illuminates it should lead us to obedience. Are you reading God's word intelligently, attentively, with the intention of obedience to what is declared? Before you begin reading, ask the Holy Spirit to reveal anything in you that needs to be changed and to give you the courage to make those changes. Walking according to God's plan will definitely bring you peace with God and the peace of God.

Father, as we study the Bible, help us to see Your direction for each day, the things we need to change in order to come into agreement with Your word and to live in complete peace.

GREAT PEACE

Great peace[H7965] have they which love thy law: and nothing shall offend[H4383] them.

Psalm 119:165

Those who love Your law have an abundance of peace, and nothing along their paths can cause them to stumble[H4383].

Psalm 119:165 (VOICE)

September 11, 2001 – Like our parents remember Pearl Harbor, December 7, 1941, our generation will never forget the day the twin towers collapsed into rubble and dust. I (Susie) was sitting at my desk in the auto dealership accounting office where I worked. My supervisor came by and asked if I'd heard the news that a plane had crashed into the World Trade Center and one of the towers was on fire. I had not because I didn't turn on the car radio that morning. Someone else came in and said, "A second plane has hit the other tower, and it looks intentional!" As my coworkers flew up the stairs to gather around the television, I sat in stunned disbelief. Realizing I was completely alone in the office, I remembered that the only and best thing I could do about this tragedy was to pray. Therefore, in the silence of the empty room, I bowed my head and asked the Lord to watch over the people in New York and to give us peace in the midst of the confusion, horror, and fear. I took a moment to call my sister who worked at a law office.

She was watching it all unfold on TV and gasped, "Oh my gosh! The tower just disintegrated!" I hung up the phone and tears flowed as I prayed for families of victims and firefighters and policemen who would risk and lose their lives. At lunch I watched news reports of a plane hitting the Pentagon and a plane ditched in a field to keep it from reaching its intended target. I prayed for wisdom for President Bush and peace for his wife. I was upset by the tragedy, but I was not unsettled. The Lord restored my peace as I exercised my faith in his sovereignty and control. Fear of more attacks gripped the nation. Reports on the radio told of local schools giving parents the option to pick up their children early. I was keenly aware that my home lay between an airbase and a major airport and only two miles from Bell Helicopter. Even with the feeling that my house had a target painted on the roof, I had to agree with our CFO when he said, "If we cease to be productive, the enemy wins." He was talking about the terrorists. I was thinking about Satan. If he could take my focus off God's power, he would win. I determined not to let him and continued to pray, and God gave me great peace.

"Offend" in this verse can be translated "cause to stumble" or "stumbling block." As long as our focus is on the Lord Jesus and demonstrating our love by trusting and obeying Him, we will not fall but will be kept in perfect peace. Things going on in our world often distract us, but we must deliberately, purposefully shift our focus away from the fear caused by circumstances and fix our gaze on Jesus, the author and finisher of our faith (Hebrews 12:2).

Father, thank You for the peace that surpasses all understanding (Phil. 4:6-7) that is ours when we cease being anxious and entrust every care to You.

Listen to and internalize Psalm 119:165, 168, 171, 172, and 175: https://www.youtube.com/watch?v=4zamjX-MDibE&list=RD4zamjXMDibE&start_radio=1

IN FAVOR OF PEACE

Woe to me that I dwell in Meshech, that I live among the tents of Kedar! Too long have I dwelt among those who hate peace^{H7965}. I am in favor of peace^{H7965}; but when I speak, they want war.

Psalm 120:5-7

120:5-7 Meshech is a reference to a people who lived far to the north of Israel, while Kedar referred to a people who lived to the southeast (120:5). Likely, then, this was his poetic way of saying that he was surrounded by those who were not God's people. (24)

The Psalmist could not possibly live in the two places he mentions because they are far apart. He is saying the people surrounding him are acting like people who do not know the one true God, acting like barbarous, cruel pagans. The psalm is a plea for God to bring about the peace he longs for. He is petitioning the God of peace to restore his inner peace as well as peace with others. He has apparently been the victim of people who answer his pleas for peace with hatred, slander, and perhaps the threat of violence. The psalm is labeled as one of several "songs of ascent" which may have been sung as a pilgrim traveled up the hill toward Jerusalem. Perhaps the psalmist is making a pilgrimage to Jerusalem, the city of "peace," to seek peace with His God as well as escape dwelling among people who are bent on disturbing his peace.

We first must establish a relationship with Father God by trusting in, relying on, the Prince of Peace, Jesus, to save us from the wrath of God. He died on the cross to pay the penalty for our sin and reconcile us to God. Once we have this peace with God, we can learn to rest in the peace of God—peace of mind and a sense of well-being and wholeness. The Apostle Paul urges us to seek peace with others, but we must realize that there are times the other person will not respond well even though we are making our best effort to live peaceably. When that happens, we must commit them to God in prayer and trust Him to change their hearts or avenge wrongs against us.

Romans 12:17-19 *Do not repay anyone evil for evil. Carefully consider what is right in the eyes of everybody. If it is possible on your part, live at peace with everyone. Do not avenge yourselves, beloved, but leave room for God's wrath. For it is written: "Vengeance is Mine; I will repay, says the Lord."*

Father, thank You that Jesus paid the price for our sins that we can have peace with You. Thank You that since we have surrendered our lives to Jesus, Your Holy Spirit lives within us and enables us to enjoy Your peace even amid difficult circumstances. Please help us to live at peace with those around us, especially fellow believers, and to be known for being in favor of peace rather than conflict.

REACTION TO TERRORISM OF SEPTEMBER 11, 2001

BY KAREN SUE HALE

PRAY FOR THE PEACE
OF JERUSALEM

Pray for the peace[H7965] of Jerusalem: "May those who love you prosper. May there be peace[H7965] within your walls, and prosperity inside your fortresses." For the sake of my brothers and friends, I will say, "Peace[H7965] be within you."

Psalm 122:6-8

122:6–9 The name "Jerusalem" means "foundation of peace," and yet the city has been a center of conflict for centuries. If we understand biblical prophecy correctly, there can be no peace in Jerusalem or on earth until the Prince of Peace reigns on David's throne (Is. 9:6, 7; Luke 1:26–33). So, when we pray for the peace of Jerusalem, we are actually praying, "Your kingdom come" (Matt. 6:10). (25)

Jerusalem is the center of the Jewish faith even though the city David prayed for and Temple his son Solomon built were eventually destroyed. The Temple rebuilt during the time of Ezra and Nehemiah also fell. Finally in A.D. 70, the Romans reduced the Temple that had been restored during the reign of King Herod to ruins. However, God's promise to Abraham remained, and all nations are blessed through his Seed which is Jesus, the Jewish Messiah. We, as Christians, still need to pray for the peace of Jerusalem. As Warren Wiersbe pointed out, Jerusalem will not truly have shalom (peace that is nothing missing, nothing broken, complete wholeness) until Jesus the Messiah, the Prince of Shalom, returns in full glory to reign and rule as King of kings and Lord of lords. Therefore, as Jesus taught His disciples, we are to pray:

Matthew 6:9b-10 *Our Father in heaven, hallowed be Your name. Your kingdom come, Your will be done, on earth as it is in heaven.*

As Christians, we still need to bless Israel because they are still God's chosen people. We need to pray for Jews to recognize that Jesus was and is the Messiah they have waited for.

> Jews are, biblically speaking, the "chosen people of God" and dearly loved by Him. Another reason for Christians to support the nation of Israel is because of the Abrahamic Covenant. We read of God's promise in Genesis 12:2-3, "I will make you into a great nation and I will bless you; I will make your name great, and you will be a blessing. I will bless those who bless you, and whoever curses you I will curse; and all peoples on earth will be blessed through you" (see also Genesis 27:29; Numbers 24:9). (26)

Numbers 24:9 (NLT) *Like a lion, Israel crouches and lies down; like a lioness, who dares to arouse her? Blessed is everyone who blesses you, O Israel, and cursed is everyone who curses you.*

Historically, the Jewish people have been persecuted, displaced from their homeland, nearly annihilated; but they continue to rise from the destruction. They are now a nation in the land God promised them. However, there is still major conflict, territory disputes, and wars. Let us remember the people of Israel in our prayers. Let us pray for the peace of Jerusalem. Let us pray, "Your kingdom come on earth as it is in Heaven."

Father, help us to remember to pray for peace in Jerusalem, for the peace of Israel. Help us to realize that their ultimate and complete peace will be ours as well because that will be when Jesus returns in all His glory and splendor.

Listen to "Sha'alu Shalom Yerushalayim/Pray for the Peace of Jerusalem - Sung by Shae Wilbur and Paul Wilbur: https://www.youtube.com/watch?v=TXKeVf4tFzQ&list=RDTXKeVf4tFzQ&start_radio=1

KEEPING COMMANDMENTS PROVIDES PEACE

My son, do not forget my teaching, but let your heart keep my commandments; for they will add length to your days, years and peace[H7965] to your life. Never let loving devotion or faithfulness leave you; bind them around your neck, write them on the tablet of your heart. Then you will find favor and high regard in the sight of God and man. Trust in the LORD with all your heart, and lean not on your own understanding; in all your ways acknowledge Him, and He will make your paths straight.

Proverbs 3:1-6

3:1–4 Throughout this chapter conditions are given for receiving God's guidance. The first condition is that we learn God's truth. The will of God is revealed in the Word of God (Col. 1:9, 10), and the only way to know His will is to study His Word and obey it. By receiving the Word within our hearts, we experience growth in godly character, so that loyalty and kindness become beautiful ornaments in our lives (Prov. 1:9; 3:3). It isn't enough for believers to carry the Bible in their hands; they must let the Holy Spirit write God's Word on their hearts (3:3; 7:3; 2 Cor. 3:1–3). Obedience to the Word can add years to our lives and life to our years. (27)

Early in my discipleship journey, I (Susie) was told to memorize specific Scripture verses to guide me. We were challenged to memorize two of them per week in the Navigator's™ discipleship program we were using. Many years later, I helped my elementary school students memorize verses by setting them to music. Two verses to memorize in your quest to follow Jesus and be conformed to His image by the Holy Spirit are:

Psalm 119:9, 11 (AMP) *How can a young man keep his way pure? By keeping watch [on himself] according to Your word [conforming his life to Your precepts]. Your word I have treasured and stored in my heart, That I may not sin against You.*

We acquire peace with God when we trust Jesus's finished work on the cross to save us from the wrath of God. That's a done deal, and we have peace with God from then on. However, to truly experience the peace of God in our lives, we need to live according to His commandments and precepts found in the Bible, not out of fear but because we love Him and want to please Him. Remember that Proverbs are a generalization. This passage does not promise we will all live to be 100 years old.

We like what Warren Wiersbe surmises at the end of the quote above that "Obedience to the Word can add years to our lives and life to our years." Susan's family was told that she would do good to live 24 years. She just celebrated her 58th birthday!!! PTL! However, that is not the biggest miracle. The greater thing God has done for her is to make those years abundant, full, and productive even though she is classified as quadriplegic. The Lord has added life to her days, and through our sistership, has added life to mine.

Try beginning each day reminding yourself of God's precepts to follow them and His promises to be encouraged. Perhaps memorize the passage above and recite it first thing in the morning. Ask Him to bring more abundant life to you each day as His Holy Spirit teaches you to be more and more like His Son, Jesus. Then your life will be not only more blessed for you, but you will be a channel of blessing to others. Our godly character will be the most attractive thing about us, even more than expensive jewelry or fancy clothing.

1 Peter 3:3-4 (VOICE) *Don't focus on decorating your exterior by doing your hair or putting on fancy jewelry or wearing fashionable clothes; let your adornment be what's inside—the real you, the lasting beauty of a gracious and quiet spirit, in which God delights.*

Father, like the old hymn says, "Make me a blessing today." When we are at peace with You and enjoy Your peace in our lives, we will live lives that overflow with love, peace, and grace to others. Please keep our focus on You and continue to conform us to the image of Christ.

John 10:10 (AMP) *The thief comes only in order to steal and kill and destroy. I came that they may have and enjoy life, and have it in abundance [to the full, till it overflows].*

Worship with the Gaither Vocal Band singing "Fully Alive":
https://www.youtube.com/watch?v=YpAeY9qqsos

Blessed is the man who finds wisdom, the man who acquires understanding, for she is more profitable than silver, and her gain is better than fine gold. She is more precious than rubies; nothing you desire compares with her. Long life is in her right hand; in her left hand are riches and honor. All her ways are pleasant, and all her paths are peaceful[H7965]. She is a tree of life to those who embrace her, and those who lay hold of her are blessed.

Proverbs 3:13-18

Proverbs 9:10 (NLT) *Fear of the LORD is the foundation of wisdom. Knowledge of the Holy One results in good judgment.*

PEACEFUL PATHS OF WISDOM

Solomon asked the Lord for wisdom,
knowing that God is her source.
Submitting to the Lord's authority
will keep us on the right course.
The wisdom that the Lord instills
is more valuable than silver or gold.
Being confident the Holy Spirit guides us
is more precious than jewels we can hold.
Wisdom leads us along peaceful paths
for the wise will follow God's ways.
Embracing wisdom makes us more like Christ
and brings blessings to all of our days.

PEACE-FILLED JOY

Deceit is in the hearts of those who devise evil, but the counselors of peace[H7965] have joy.

Proverbs 12:20

In order to be someone who encourages peace, one must intentionally and deliberately emulate the Prince of Peace. If you squeeze a lemon, lemon juice pours from it. If you squeeze a Christian, the Fruit of the Spirit should flow from him or her. Two of the Fruit of the Spirit are peace and joy (Galatians 5:22-23). The Lord encourages those who strive for peace in the Beatitudes when He says, "Blessed are the peacemakers, for they will be called sons of God" (Matthew 5:9).

During my month-long hospital adventure to have both my legs amputated above the knee, I (Susan) knew intense fear and anxiety. The challenge was to overcome them and not be overcome by them. Those emotions had to be subdued by the Prince of Peace in order for me to effectively share His gospel. Praise the Lord, He had already given instructions for replacing anxiety with peace:

Philippians 4:6-7 *Be anxious for nothing, but in everything, by prayer and petition, with thanksgiving, present your requests to God. And the peace of God, which surpasses all understanding, will guard your hearts and your minds in Christ Jesus.*

God's grace was paramount during the trial, the peace of God overshadowing my difficult situation. God brought people of differing faiths to my bedside and enabled me to share His love even in the midst of my pain. I pray that through my testimony, they may find the perfect peace that comes only from trusting the Lord Jesus Christ and discover true joy that is not dependent upon circumstances.

When anxious thoughts begin to well up inside you, immediately bring them to the Lord in prayer, thanking Him in advance for His watchful care for you. He will grant you peace as you trust Him even in the storms of life. He will enable you to have peace-filled joy when you "Cast all your anxiety on Him, because He cares for you" (I Peter 5:7).

Father, we thank You that Your peace enables us to exude joy even during difficult situations. Thank You for holding us securely in Your hand.

Remember that Jesus is with you always, even in the eye of the storm. Perhaps you have experienced His peace when all around you is not peaceful. If so, you can relate to "Eye of the Storm" sung by Ryan Stevenson: https://www.youtube.com/watch?v=X2FqFLKisys

ENEMIES LIVE
AT PEACE WITH US

When a man's ways please the LORD, He makes even the man's enemies live at peace[H7999] with him.

Proverbs 16:7

This is the first time we have seen a slightly different Hebrew word for peace. It is still a derivative of "shalom," but the word used here seems to indicate feeling safe because there is a peace treaty in effect. The context is that God causes there to be peace between the man and his enemies.

> H7999. šālam: A verb meaning to be safe, to be completed. The primary meaning is to be safe or uninjured in mind or body (Job 8:6; 9:4). This word is normally used when God is keeping His people safe. In its simple form, this verb also means to be completed or to be finished. This could refer to something concrete such as a building (1 Kgs. 7:51); or things more abstract, such as plans (Job 23:14). Other meanings of this verb include to be at peace with another person (Ps. 7:4[5]); to make a treaty of peace (Josh. 11:19; Job 5:23); to pay, to give a reward (Ps. 62:12[13]); to restore, repay, or make retribution (Ex. 21:36; Ps. 37:21). (28)

16:7 please the Lord. Following God's way has reconciling and healing effects on personal relationships. (29)

7 Peaceful conduct. The subject matter of the verse is "a man's ways" that are "pleasing" to the Lord. The question is: who is the subject of the second clause? The appropriate choice is the "man" and his "ways"—it is his godly lifestyle that disarms the enemies. A life that pleases God will be above reproach and find favor with others. This is part of God's plan for rewards. But we must remember that like many proverbs, this one must not be pressed to universal applications (cf. 2Ti 3:12 for a contrasting statement). (30)

2 Timothy 3:12 (ESV) *Indeed, all who desire to live a godly life in Christ Jesus will be persecuted . . .*

We are only able to please God when we know Him intimately because we have trusted in His Son Jesus to reconcile us to the Father. His Holy Spirit empowers us to choose obedience on a daily basis. The Holy Spirit enables us to live a life pleasing to God, but we still have the responsibility to wisely choose to follow His prompting.

John 15:5 *I am the vine and you are the branches. The one who remains in Me, and I in him, will bear much fruit. For apart from Me you can do nothing.*

When we surrender control to the Holy Spirit who lives within us as Christ-followers, we will exhibit the Fruit of the Spirit: love, joy, peace, patience, kindness, goodness, faithfulness, gentleness, and self-control (Galatians 5:22-23). These character traits can disarm our enemies as God uses them to touch their hearts. As pointed out above, there will be those who are determined to persecute believers. However, in our daily interactions with our neighbors, co-workers, etc., our consistent walk with the Lord will enable us to live at peace.

How can our ways please the Lord? They are pleasing to Him when we walk in His ways. Perhaps we can begin each day by praying along with the psalmist: "Show me Your ways, O LORD; teach me Your paths." (Psalm 25:4) and obeying what He reveals to us.

Father, help us to consistently walk in Your ways and stay on the path You have chosen for us. Grow us up to look more and more like Jesus in our conduct. Thank You for placing Your Spirit within us to guide us.

SAR SHALOM: PRINCE OF PEACE

For unto us a child is born, unto us a son is given, and the government will be upon His shoulders. And He will be called Wonderful Counselor, Mighty God, Everlasting Father, Prince of Peace.

Isaiah 9:6

A child is born—manger, star, shepherds, wise men— the nativity scene in the church pageant. Tiny Baby with huge responsibilities. Let's explore just one of His titles: Prince of Peace or in the Hebrew, Sar Shalom. We all know what a prince is, but what is the complete meaning of shalom? Shalom is translated peace but is not necessarily the absence of strife. It is peace in the sense of being whole, being well, even in the middle of unsettling circumstances. It is being immovable, unshakable when the world seems to be collapsing around you. Psalm 62:6, "He only is my rock and my salvation: he is my defense; I shall not be moved." When Jesus was born in Bethlehem, it was not to bring peace to the nations, although when He returns all men will be at peace (Micah 4:3). He did not even promise immediate peace between individuals because, as we know, the price of becoming a Christian is often the loss of even family relationships (Matthew 10:33-35). What Jesus accomplished in the incarnation and His time on earth as the God-Man was to announce the Kingdom of God and purchase our redemption on the cross. The price He paid enables us to live at peace with God and to have His peace within us. Jesus promised to leave His peace with those who believe, "Peace I leave with you, my peace I give unto you: not as the world giveth, give I unto you. Let not your heart be troubled, neither let it be afraid" (John 14:27). The apostle Paul described this shalom in Philippians 4:6-7, "Be careful for nothing; but in every-thing by prayer and supplication with thanksgiving let your requests be made known unto God. And the peace of God, which passes all understanding, shall keep your hearts and minds through Christ Jesus." Because we are at peace with God and have His unshakable peace in our hearts, we can make the effort to be at peace with others (Romans 12:18), thereby exhibiting this fruit of the Spirit.

Even though we are certain of our peace with God because of the price Jesus paid to offer us the gift of freedom from God's wrath, we sometimes struggle with maintaining the peace of God in our daily lives. How can we rest in the peace that the Prince of Peace provides? Challenge yourself to memorize key verses dealing with our peace of mind such as Philippians 4:6-7, John 14:27, and 1 Peter 5:7. A great verse to memorize from the old testament:

Isaiah 26:3 *You will keep in perfect peace all who trust in you, all whose thoughts are fixed on you!*

Shift your focus to and memorize the following list:

Philippians 4:8 (NLT) *And now, dear brothers and sisters, one final thing. Fix your thoughts on what is true, and honorable, and right, and pure, and lovely, and admirable. Think about things that are excellent and worthy of praise.*

Jesus, Prince of Peace, thank You for filling our hearts with Your peace even when circumstances tempt us to panic and doubt that peace. Help us to focus on Your promises concerning peace of mind.

Listen to Isaiah 9:6-7 from Handel's "Messiah" being sung by the Warsaw Philharmonic Orchestra and Choir, Haselböck directing:
https://www.youtube.com/watch?v=CHK8hJ22SP-w&list=RDCHK8hJ22SPw&start_radio=1

EVERLASTING KINGDOM OF PEACE

Of the increase of His government and peace[H7965] there will be no end. He will reign on the throne of David and over his kingdom, to establish and sustain it with justice and righteousness from that time and forevermore. The zeal of the LORD of Hosts will accomplish this.

Isaiah 9:7

His leadership will bring such prosperity as you've never seen before— sustainable peace[H7965] for all time. This child: God's promise to David—a throne forever, among us, to restore sound leadership that cannot be perverted or shaken. He will ensure justice without fail and absolute equity. Always. The intense passion of the Eternal, Commander of heavenly armies, will carry this to completion.

Isaiah 9:7 (VOICE)

When Jesus returns to reign eternally, He will fulfill God's promise that's David's throne would be established forever. He will reign with complete justice and righteousness. For those of us who have surrendered our lives to the Lord and trusted in Jesus alone to save us from God's wrath and eternal separation from His goodness, there will be no fear of that justice because we have been washed in the soap of His love, His redeeming blood. We wear the righteousness of Jesus like a garment.

Isaiah 61:10 (VOICE) *I am filled with joy and my soul vibrates with exuberant hope, because of the Eternal my God; For He has dressed me with the garment of salvation, wrapped me with the robe of righteousness. It's as though I'm dressed for my wedding day, in the very best: a bridegroom's garland and a bride's jewels.*

Philippians 3:9b *I no longer count on my own righteousness through obeying the law; rather, I become righteous through faith in Christ. For God's way of making us right with himself depends on faith.*

The proper terminology is that Christ's righteousness is imputed to our account:

IMPU'TED, participle passive Charged to the account of; attributed; ascribed. (31)

There is no way we could be perfect enough to earn our way to Heaven. God gives a gift when we place our trust in Jesus to impute all the goodness, all the righteousness of the only perfect Man to our account. We are citizens of that Kingdom, the bride that Jesus as our bridegroom has prepared to enter His father's house.

Philippians 3:20-21 *But our citizenship is in heaven, and we eagerly await a Savior from there, the Lord Jesus Christ, who, by the power that enables Him to subject all things to Himself, will transform our lowly bodies to be like His glorious body.*

Ephesians 5:25-27 *Husbands, love your wives, just as Christ loved the church and gave Himself up for her to sanctify her, cleansing her by the washing with water through the word, and to present her to Himself as a glorious church, without stain or wrinkle or any such blemish, but holy and blameless.*

God's intense passion for His people, those who trust in Jesus, will bring about this everlasting Kingdom of complete righteousness, justice, and peace. Are you certain that eternal peace is your final destination? If not, turn to the "Jewels of Salvation" section in the back of this book or reach out to us via email at SRSlade2009@gmail.com. We would love to tell you more about God's saving grace!

Father, we look forward with expectant, enthusiastic hope to the triumphant return of Jesus and spending eternity with our Bridegroom in the place He has prepared for us. (John 14).

KEPT IN PERFECT PEACE

You will keep in perfect peace^{H7965} all who trust in you, all whose thoughts are fixed^{H5564} on you! Trust in the Lord always, for the Lord God is the eternal Rock.
Isaiah 26:3-4 (NLT)

> H5564 çâmak, saw-mak'; a primitive root; to prop (literally or figuratively); reflexively, to lean upon or take hold of (in a favorable or unfavorable sense):—bear up, establish, (up-) hold, lay, lean, lie hard, put, rest self, set self, stand fast, stay (self), sustain. (32)

The Hebrew word translated "fixed" can mean to be propped up, leaning upon, resting on the object which in this case is the Lord. When we are "fixed" on Jesus, it is as if we are super-glued to Him. Peace and rest go hand in hand. When we experience perfect peace, we can relax and rest because we are free from fear or concern. Rest is not always cessation from activity, but rather not feeling frantic in our activity. This is the result of an intimate relationship with our Savior, our Rock, Jesus.

Peace is not necessarily the absence of turmoil. It is relying on Christ as He takes you through the storm, not being moved from your faith by difficult circumstances.

How can we grasp hold of this type of peace? Isaiah 26:3 tells us that our thoughts need to be fixed on the Lord, cemented to Him. How do we do this? As we have stated before, memorize God's promises regarding your peace of mind. Think on God's goodness and lean on His truth.

Something that helps both of us refocus our thoughts in times of trouble is worshiping the Lord in song or even listening to songs about His faithfulness, His peace, He mightiness. For example, listen and maybe sing along with the Gaither Vocal Band since the lyrics are provided as they worship Him wholeheartedly with the song "My Feet Are on the Rock."
https://www.youtube.com/watch?v=NmKxCCfwBjc

Father, we thank You for Your word and for those who write songs that help us internalize truths from Your word. Help us, especially during difficult times, to focus our thoughts on Your unchanging grace.

BEAUTIFUL FEET

How beautiful on the mountains are the feet of those who bring good news, who proclaim peace[H7965], who bring good tidings, who proclaim salvation, who say to Zion, "Your God reigns!"

Isaiah 52:7

In Isaiah's time, the feet of him who brings good news referred to a messenger announcing a great deed, usually a military victory. Paul quotes 52:7 in Rom. 10:15, as he urges believers to spread the good news of salvation in Christ, freely available for all peoples around the globe. The word "gospel" means "good news." (33)

Romans 10:15 *And how can they preach unless they are sent? As it is written: "How beautiful are the feet of those who bring good news!"*

...the spread of the gospel of Jesus Christ among all the nations of the earth by evangelists and missionaries is seen by the apostle Paul in Romans 10:15 as a direct fulfillment of verse 7. (34)

Ephesians 6:15 (NLT) *For shoes, put on the peace that comes from the Good News so that you will be fully prepared.*

When I look at my feet, the word "beautiful" certainly does NOT come to mind. I have scars on both feet, my toes cross on top of each other, and I do not wear sandals anymore. Now Susan might chime in that she no longer has feet! However, the beauty comes from being messengers of the Lord to bring good news to people everywhere. What is this good news? For Isaiah, the immediate good news was that the Jews would return to Israel and rebuild Zion (a.k.a. Jerusalem) which came to pass under Ezra's leadership. Currently (2025), the "good news" is the Gospel of Jesus Christ. In a nutshell, the good news is that God came to earth in the form of His Son, Jesus, and was born as a human baby: fully man, but fully God. He lived a perfect, sinless life among humankind and taught those who followed Him about God's kingdom. He died on the cross to satisfy the wrath of God toward our sin, in essence paying the debt we owed. By His suffering the death penalty that should have been ours, He gave us access to God and eternal life with Him. Jesus rose from the grave and is alive today interceding for us at the right hand of the throne of God. Those who have chosen to believe this good news and place their trust in Jesus, surrendering control of their lives to Him, receive His Holy Spirit to teach them, guide them, comfort them, and lead them to live more abundantly.

Ask yourself, "Are my feet beautiful?" The answer is that if you are telling others about the love of Jesus and sharing His good news with them, they are! Paul even included our feet in the armor of the Lord he wrote about in Ephesians 6. The peace that comes from knowing and accepting the Gospel, the good news, are the army boots that help us to stand firm when circumstances try to rob us of our peace! These boots are designed to fit all believers: young or old, tiny or tall, male or female. Somehow, even Susan can put on these boots!!!

Father, help us to be messengers that proclaim the Good News of peace and salvation unashamedly and boldly! Help us to have beautiful feet!

Worship opportunity: Worship with Twila Paris singing her original song "How Beautiful": https://www.youtube.com/watch?v=jVu5VZsCNOI

Surely He took on our infirmities and carried our sorrows; yet we considered Him stricken by God, struck down and afflicted. But He was pierced for our transgressions, He was crushed for our iniquities; the punishment that brought us peace[H7965] was upon Him, and by His stripes we are healed. We all like sheep have gone astray, each one has turned to his own way; and the LORD has laid upon Him the iniquity of us all.

Isaiah 53:4-6

53:5-6 These verses couldn't more clearly depict what Jesus Christ endured. The use of language is precise regarding the kind of death he would die (he was pierced) and the reason for it (because of our iniquities) (53:5). He was punished . . . for the iniquity of us all. Hundreds of years before it would happen, the prophet testified to the substitutionary atonement of Christ on the cross. (35)

SUFFERING SERVANT BRINGS SHALOM

Christ took on our infirmities
and carried all our sorrows.
He was pierced for our transgressions
as He died upon the tree.

The punishment He suffered
was the sentence we deserved.
Jesus died as our substitute,
from sin's prison set us free.

Like sheep we wandered far from God,
each living "my way."
Jesus, our Good Shepherd, died
as the perfect, spotless Lamb.

By His death, He bought
our shalom with God—wholeness,
Nothing broken, nothing missing—
reconciled to the Great I Am.

Worship Jesus as you listen to "Man of Sorrows" written
by Phillip P. Bliss and sung by the Gaither Vocal Band:
https://www.youtube.com/watch?v=IL9hckqmcGo

LED FORTH IN PEACE

You will indeed go out with joy and be led forth in peace[H7965]; the mountains and hills will burst into song before you, and all the trees of the field will clap their hands.

Isaiah 55:12

Paraphrasing only verse 12 from Isaiah 55–a chapter rich with invitation, comfort, and wisdom–Steffi G. Rubin (b. The Bronx, NY, 1950) wrote "The Trees of the Field" in 1975. Verse 12 refers to the "going out" from Babylon, the Israelites' return from exile. More generally, and certainly as seen through New Testament eyes, the passage sings of the joy resulting from God's salvation, a joy so far-reaching that even the "trees of the field will clap their hands," and fruitful trees and bushes will grow instead of thorns and briers. . . The song's popularity is no doubt due to the Jewish-style music by Stuart Dauermann (b. Brooklyn, NY, 1944). Both text and tune were written for the Liberated Wailing Wall, the touring singing group of Jews for Jesus. It was first published in Scriptures to Sing (Lillenas, 1975). (36)

Prophecy often has a near interpretation and one that applies to future events. Isaiah was writing about the eventual return of the Israelites from captivity in

Babylon which was indeed a joyous occasion with celebration and singing. However, the later interpretation can be applied to the freedom and peace we experience as those saved by faith in Jesus by the grace of God. The Israelites were looking forward to a time of peace in their homeland. Those of us who follow Jesus experience peace with God which leads to the peace of God, an inner, calm confidence that our Good Shepherd is watching over us.

There are many external forces that try to rob us of our peace: job stress, family crises, financial problems, poor health, etc. However, when turmoil arises on any front, we can turn our attention to Jesus by focusing on Scripture verses that assure us of His peace. Have you committed any of those to memory? Start with these:

Philippians 4:6-7 *Be anxious for nothing, but in everything, by prayer and petition, with thanksgiving, present your requests to God. And the peace of God, which surpasses all understanding, will guard your hearts and your minds in Christ Jesus.*

John 14:17 *Peace I leave with you; My peace I give to you. I do not give to you as the world gives. Do not let your hearts be troubled; do not be afraid.*

Try praying God's word back to Him.

Father, there are many circumstances going on right now that could cause us to be anxious. We thank You because we know You have it all under control and pray that You would replace our anxieties with Your perfect peace. Lord, Jesus, You promised Your disciples that You were leaving them Your peace. We, too, are Your disciples. Therefore, we turn our troubled hearts to You and trust that You will remove our fear and replace it with that peace.

Worship along with "The Trees of the Field will Clap Their Hands" sung by the Gaither Homecoming Friends during visit to Israel: https://www.youtube.com/watch?v=cjL27TlSwYU

PEACEMAKERS LOOK LIKE PAPA

Blessed (enjoying enviable happiness, spiritually pros-
perous—with life-joy and satisfaction in God's favor
and salvation, regardless of their outward conditions)
are the makers and maintainers of peace[G1518], for they
shall be called the sons of God!

Matthew 5:9 (AMPC)

I (Susan) see many corollaries between the Beatitudes and the Fruit of the Spirit (Galatians 5:22-23). Both the Beatitudes and the Fruit of the Spirit are a result of our relationship to Christ and not the way to establish that relationship. Our salvation is completely accomplished by God's grace, and the works we exhibit are the result of our submission to Him. The Fruit of the Spirit flows through us to others when we have committed and submitted our lives to God's will for us rather than our own will. The Beatitudes and the Fruit of the Spirit are an outflow of our BEING God's children rather than striving to DO works. When we are at peace with the Father, He enables us to make the effort to be at peace with others (Romans 12:18). Being peacemakers not only brings us the benefit of blessing (having a joy-filled life no matter what the circumstances around us may be), but also causes others to see the Father in us. We have a friend whose son looks more like his clone. Pictures of them at the same ages look almost like identical twins! He could never deny that he is that son's father. We are being made more and more to look like Jesus (Romans

8:29) who is the exact representation of His Father (Hebrews 1:3). Peacemakers will be called the children of God. We are to exhibit His characteristics so that others will know we have been adopted into God's family. We are to look more and more like our Papa. God created people in His image (Genesis 1:26), but that image was tarnished by sin. As the Holy Spirit changes us from the inside out, He removes that tarnish, that stain, and polishes us to look more and more like the Father, to be a reflection of Papa's attributes.

When people look at you, not just on the outside but really examine your life, do you resemble our Heavenly Father? Or as the old hymn admonishes us, "Let Others See Jesus in You." Take a moment to listen to it being sung by John McKay:
https://www.youtube.com/watch?v=nomNLqN9Sw0

Father, thank You for sending Your Son Jesus to die for us even when we were tarnished by sin. Thank You for infusing us with the Holy Spirit who works within us to remove the stains and make us more and more like You.

PEACE, BE STILL

And he arose, and rebuked the wind, and said unto the sea, Peace^{G4623}, be still. And the wind ceased, and there was a great calm. And he said unto them, Why are ye so fearful? how is it that ye have no faith? And they feared exceedingly, and said one to another, What manner of man is this, that even the wind and the sea obey him?
Mark 4:39 (KJV)

And He got up and [sternly] rebuked the wind and said to the sea, "Hush^{G4623,} be still (muzzled)!" And the wind died down [as if it had grown weary] and there was [at once] a great calm [a perfect peacefulness].
Mark 4:39 (AMP)

G4623 *siōpáō*, see-o-pah'-o; from siōpé (silence, i.e. a hush; properly, muteness, i.e. involuntary stillness, or inability to speak; and thus differing from G4602, which is rather a voluntary refusal or indisposition to speak, although the terms are often used synonymously); to be dumb (but not deaf also, like G2974 properly); figuratively, to be calm (as quiet water):—dumb, (hold) peace. (37) (Strong's)

When Jesus emerged from the hold of the ship, He exercised divine power over His creation (cf. Col. 1:16). The word for "rebuke" (see Mark 4:39) means "to express strong disapproval of someone," "reprove," or "censure." Jesus hushed the storm like a parent reprimands a toddler throwing a tantrum. Unlike a rebellious child, however, the wind and waves obeyed. Immediately. (38)

Jesus put the wind and the waves in a divine time-out. It's like the wind and the waves were two small children arguing. When a classroom of children is excessively noisy, the teacher sometimes flips the light switch a couple of times, and the children cease talking immediately. Jesus brought a hush, a serene quiet, a complete peace in the middle of a storm simply by speaking to the waves and the wind. He exhibited complete control over the forces of nature. This opened the disciples' eyes to the fact that Jesus was more than just a man.

If Jesus can control the forces of nature, bringing peace in the middle of a storm, surely, He can command peace during our stress storms. Our inner turmoil or emotional upheaval is no match for the Master. Jesus can bring peace in the middle of our unrest. When circumstances seem insurmountable and unrelenting, take a deep breath and pray. Ask the Lord to give you peace of mind and reassure you that He is in control. Exchange frantic fear for the powerful presence of the Lord.

Father, help us to practice what we suggest to others. In the middle of our own concerns, help us to trust that You control all circumstances and will use every trial for our good and Your glory. Enable us to be still and know that You are God! (Psalm 46:10).

Worship with Hope Darst singing "Peace, Be Still": https://www.youtube.com/watch?v=lsIpGiz3S-fQ&list=RDlsIpGiz3SfQ&start_radio=1

GO IN PEACE AND BE FREE

Then the woman, knowing what had happened to her, came and fell down before Him trembling in fear, and she told Him the whole truth. "Daughter," said Jesus, "your faith has healed[G4982] you. Go in peace[G1515] and be free[G5199] of your affliction."

Mark 5:33-34 (see also Luke 8:47-48)

You may or may not know the rest of the story. This woman had been having an issue of blood for twelve years. Doctors had been unable to cure her, and she had spent a fortune on them. She was in a crowd watching Jesus and His disciples as they were on their way to house of Jairus to heal his sick daughter. She came up to Jesus and touched the "hem of his garment." However, the Complete Jewish Study Bible translates it this way:

Luke 8:44 (CJB) *came up behind him and touched the tzitzit on his robe; instantly her hemorrhaging stopped.*

You may have noticed the Hebrew word 'tzitzit" in the Complete Jewish Bible translation of Luke 8:44 above. This word referred to the fringe on the edge of a garment to remind the Jewish people to obey God (Numbers 15:38-40, Deuteronomy 22:12). What the note in the CJB translation pointed out was that this fringe was also referred to as "the wings" of the garment. Since the woman who had been bleeding for twelve years probably knew the prophecy of Malachi 4:2, it would make sense for her to reach out to touch Jesus's "wings". By doing so, she was demonstrating faith that Jesus was, indeed, the Messiah of God who had "healing in His wings."

Malachi 4:2 (KJV) *But unto you that fear my name shall the Sun of righteousness arise with healing in his wings; and ye shall go forth, and grow up as calves of the stall.*

For the woman, her malady–the bleeding—was the biggest issue; but Jesus dealt with her biggest need—deliverance from the sin that separated her from God. He called her "daughter," which recognized that He accepted her faith in Him as the Messiah, and she was now a part of the family of God. Note that the Greek word translated "healed" can also mean "saved, delivered, or made whole." The woman demonstrated her faith that Jesus was the Messiah by acting on the prophecy of Malachi 4:2. Therefore, she was demonstrating saving faith. The second reference to healing, "free of your affliction" could be translated "healthy". Jesus addressed the entirety of her needs, not just the problem that was troubling her at the time.

> G4982 sốzō; fut. sốsō, aor. pass. esốthēn, perf. pass. sésōsmai, from sốs (n.f.), safe, delivered. To save, deliver, make whole, preserve safe from danger, loss, destruction. (39)

> G5199 *hugiếs*; gen. hugioús, masc.–fem., neut.

hugiés, adj. Sound, healthy. In the NT, sound, whole, in health (Matt. 12:13; 15:31; Mark 3:5; 5:34; Luke 6:10; John 5:4, 6, 9, 11, 14, 15; 7:23; Acts 4:10). (40)

The woman can truly "go in peace" because she knows she is at peace with God from this encounter with the Messiah as well as being made completely well of her bleeding disorder.

Physical healing does not always occur even when we have complete faith that Jesus is able to deliver us from our health challenges. However, we can rest, be at peace, knowing that we belong to Jesus as part of His forever family when we have placed our trust Him. Until the time that we are healed physically, we must rely on Him to walk with us through our suffering. We also have the hope—the assurance and confidence—that no matter how much pain we have while in our "earth-suits," it will pale in comparison to the intense joy and monumental glory we will experience for eternity.

2 Corinthians 4:16-18 *Therefore we do not lose heart. Though our outer self is wasting away, yet our inner self is being renewed day by day. For our light and momentary affliction is producing for us an eternal glory that is far beyond comparison. So we fix our eyes not on what is seen, but on what is unseen. For what is seen is temporary, but what is unseen is eternal....*

Father, when our pain is intense and our suffering feels immense and endless, please help us to focus on the joy and peace that You have in store for us when we are united with You in Glory, never to be separated, continually to live in complete wholeness and health.

Listen to "The woman with the issue of blood: a story of faith" from New Christian Songs: https://www.youtube.com/watch?v=BzPpc9a_5k8&list=RDBzPpc9a_5k8&start_radio=1

PEACE PRESERVERS

Salt is good, but if the salt loses its saltiness, with what will you season it? Have salt among yourselves, and be at peace[G1514] with one another."

Mark 9:50

9:50 Salt is good. Salt was an essential item in first-century Palestine. In a hot climate, without refrigeration, salt was the practical means of preserving food. Have salt in yourselves. The work of the Word (Col. 3:16) and the Spirit (Gal. 5:22, 23) produce godly character, enabling a person to act as a preservative in society. (41)

9:50 Have salt in yourselves. The image of salt describes true discipleship. Salt is a preservative. Jesus is telling His disciples to use humility and service to preserve the peace of the church, rather than dividing it through a desire to be great (v. 34). (42)

1514. *eirēneúō*; fut. eirēneúsō, from eirḗnē (1515), peace. To make peace, be at peace (1 Kgs. 22:44). In the NT metaphorically to live in peace, harmony, accord. Used in an absolute sense in 2 Cor. 13:11. In 1 Thess. 5:13, "be at peace among yourselves"; Mark 9:50, "with each other" (a.t.); Rom. 12:18, "with all." (43)

When the Holy Spirit grows the Fruit of the Spirt— love, joy, peace, patience, kindness, goodness, faithfulness, gentleness, and self-control—in our lives, He is increasing our saltiness. These Christ-like characteristics serve as a witness to those who do not yet know Jesus; but they also help us to preserve peace within the *familyship* of God. We are to are to live in harmony with our brothers and sisters in Christ which can only be achieved through humility and willingness to serve each other.

Examine your own attitudes and actions toward other believers. Are you consistently working to preserve peace within the body of Christ? Are there areas where your saltiness may be a bit week? Ask the Lord to show you specific ways to improve your spiritual sodium content by practicing and working to preserve peace in your relationships with brothers and sisters in Christ.

Father, as we study the Fruit of the Spirit, we are seeing how each one builds on the others and that developing these attributes not only improves our relationship with You but also our relationships with others. Please help us to be people who preserve peace and not those who disturb it.

PROPHET TO PREPARE THE WAY FOR THE PRINCE OF PEACE

And you, child, will be called a prophet of the Most High; for you will go on before the Lord to prepare the way for Him, to give to His people the knowledge of salvation through the forgiveness of their sins, because of the tender mercy of our God, by which the Dawn[G395] will visit us from on high, to shine on those who live in darkness and in the shadow of death, to guide our feet into the path of peace[G1515].

Luke 1:76-79 (Malachi 3:1; Isaiah 40:3 Isaiah 9:2)

Malachi 3:1 (BSB) *"Behold, I will send My messenger, who will prepare the way before Me. Then the Lord whom you seek will suddenly come to His temple—the Messenger of the covenant, in whom you delight—see, He is coming," says the LORD of Hosts.*

Zachariah was not only pronouncing a blessing on his son, John, but was declaring a prophecy concerning his future. John the Baptist would be the forerunner of the Messiah, the preface to the Living Word, that Isaiah had written about centuries earlier:

Isaiah 40:3 (NLT) *Listen! It's the voice of someone shouting, "Clear the way through the wilderness for the LORD! Make a straight highway through the wasteland for our God!*

The "Dawn" is a reference to the Messiah, who is the Light that shines in the darkness. Israel had been subject to Rome and their king, Herod, was Rome's puppet. It was indeed a dark, shadowy time. John the Baptist's birth signaled that the Light would soon burst upon the scene, and no one could extinguish it.

> G395. *anatolé*; gen. anatolés, fem. noun from anatéllō (393), to rise. The dayspring or dawn, used only in a spiritual sense (Luke 1:78). (44)

John 1:5 (NLT) *The light shines in the darkness, and the darkness can never extinguish it.*

Malachi 4:2 (NLT) *"But for you who fear my name, the Sun of Righteousness will rise with healing in his wings. And you will go free, leaping with joy like calves let out to pasture.*

> Malachi 4:2 Calves, when confined to a stall for extended periods of time, leap for sheer joy when turned loose into the sunlight. The picture is one of a joyful, vigorous, and carefree life. (45)

Jesus, the Messiah, the Prince of Peace, would bring joy and peace to all who trusted in Him. The thing about the calves was puzzling until we realized they had been set free from their stalls to graze, run, and play in the pasture, like a baby cow dance party! Jesus sets us free from our bondage to sin—anything that separates us from Holy God. We should be singing and shouting and maybe even leaping with joy. Do you have that peace with God that Jesus died to provide for you? If not, or if you are not sure, please read the Jewels of Salvation in the back of this book. Or if you prefer, contact us through our website, www.preciousjewelsministries.com, if you have questions or need to solidify your understanding of surrendering your life to Jesus.

Father, help us to never take our peace with You for granted! Let us rejoice in the fact that we are set free from the bondage of sin, that which deserves the exacting of Your righteous wrath, because Jesus died in our place. May that truth give us peace that saturates our being even in the middle of our trials.

Ever wonder what Zachariah's song would sound like in Hebrew? Here is! Listen to "A Star is Born-Zachariah's Song" by the Messianic Jewish Alliance of Israel: https://www.youtube.com/results?search_query=Zachariah%27s+song

PEACE ON EARTH

And suddenly there appeared with the angel a great multitude of the heavenly host, praising God and saying: "Glory to God in the highest, and on earth peace^{G1515} *to men on whom His favor*^{G2107} *rests!"*

Luke 2:13-14

G2107. *eudokía*; gen. eudokías, fem. noun from eudokéō (2106), to please, favor. Good will, good pleasure, good intent, benevolence, a gracious purpose (Matt. 11:26; Luke 10:21). In this sense it is parallel to eulogía (2129), blessing. Eudokía must be an outcome of agathōsúnē (19), goodness, the virtue of beneficence even as works are the product of faith. Therefore, the eudokía, the good will of agathōsúnē, denotes that which pleases, goodness, the tendency to the good.
(I) Particular delight in any person or thing and hence good will, favor (Luke 2:14, "good will toward men" on the part of God; (46)

When the Lord's redemptive plan is complete, He will have restored peace between God and humanity (Rom. 5:1), as well as peace between all individuals. The phrase "with whom He is pleased" comes from a single Greek word, eudokia [2107], which is notoriously difficult to translate. It is loosely based on a classical Greek verb meaning "to take pleasure or delight in" but is otherwise not found anywhere outside biblical literature. Eudokia appears to have been coined by the translators of the Septuagint to render some instances of the Hebrew term rātson [H7522], which often implies divine grace (Pss. 5:12; 51:18; 106:4).

The NASB rendering vaguely suggests that something in humanity pleased God, prompting Him to reward us with His favor. The NIV translation, "on whom his favor rests," captures the expression a little better. Based on no particular merit of our own, God delighted to grace humanity with a Savior. (47)

Obviously, Jesus's incarnation did not immediately bring peace between people or nations as there have perpetually been numerous wars, feuds, and disagreements since the time of Christ. That peace will only happen when He returns to rule and reign in power eternally. The peace on earth that was made available to all people is the peace with God that is ours when we surrender our lives to Jesus. We do not receive this peace by "pleasing God"—in other words, good deeds or works. God is pleased to graciously bestow that peace on us as His gift when we trust in Jesus's finished work on the cross and surrender to His will for our lives.

The angels were announcing the birth of the One who would bring peace. Have you trusted in Jesus to bring you peace with God—freedom from the fear of His anger—and the peace of God—tranquility even in the storms of everyday life? If you have that peace, take a moment to thank God and praise Him! If not, you may have it today! Talk to a Bible preaching pastor, a Christian friend, or even us! You may email us at SRSlade2009@gmail.com.

Father, we thank You for Your benevolence toward us that even though we do not deserve it, You granted us salvation and peace!

Worship the Prince of Peace along with the Gaither Vocal Band singing "Gloria": https://www.youtube.com/watch?v=vuxTECzljzI

Glory to God in the highest, and on earth peace, good will toward men.

Luke 2:14

I sent this poem in with my son's Christmas card when he was serving in Iraq. Praise the Lord, he's home now! We included it to remind us all to pray for those sons and daughters still serving around the world this Christmas.- *Susie*

CHRISTMAS POEM BY A SOLDIER'S MOM

Peace on earth, good will toward men,
tidings of comfort and joy...
These words seem trite in the Christmas cards
to send to Iraq to my boy.
But I know that the peace we have in this world
is a peace that settles within
when we trust in our heavenly Father
and the power that comes from Him.
The Lord has sent us His good will
in His ambassador, His Son,
who from the cross cried "It is finished!"
His mission on earth was done.
Tidings of comfort God brings to me
as I pray for my soldier boy.

God's only Son was sent on a mission,
so I can share tidings of joy.
He's no longer the Babe in the manger...
He's my rock, my fortress, my defense;
and knowing my son is in His loving hands
overcomes fears most immense.
Peace on earth, good will toward men,
tidings of comfort and joy...
I no longer hesitate to send that card
to Iraq to my soldier boy.

SHALOM FOR SIMEON

Sovereign Lord, as You have promised, You now dismiss Your servant in peace^{G1515}. For my eyes have seen Your salvation, which You have prepared in the sight of all people, a light for revelation to the Gentiles, and for glory to Your people Israel.

Luke 2:29-32

Isaiah 25:9 (ESV) *And it shall be said in that day, Lo, this is our God; we have waited for him, and he will save us: this is the Lord; we have waited for him, we will be glad and rejoice in his salvation.*

Simeon means "obedient, listening." Because he was obedient to have his heart tuned to the Lord and knew God's word, Simeon heard the Spirit in his heart assuring him he would live to see the Messiah. Somehow the Spirit prompted him to go to the temple that very day and hour that Jesus was being dedicated. There he saw baby Jesus in his parents' arms and KNEW by the Spirit's revelations this infant was the Son of God. He was filled with hope, peace, and comfort. Joy overwhelmed him as he took the Baby into his arms to bless him. Simeon had been promised he would see the Messiah before he died. Simeon believed the Lord was sovereign and kept His promises, but now he had seen the Lord's Promised One with his own eyes. Simeon's psalm is known as the "Nunc Dimittis" (Now You dismiss) from the first two words of the Latin translation. Now he could rest in peace, God could dismiss him from his service. He had been allowed to see the promised Hope, our freedom—the chain breaker, the One who delivers us from the prison of sin. He also acknowledged in his speech that Jesus was not for Israel alone. He was to make the message available to other nations, Gentiles included. Simeon referred to the Messiah as a light, and in the gospel of John, we saw that Jesus is The Light (John chapter 1). Jesus Himself said that He was The Light:

John 8:12 (BSB) *Again Jesus spoke to them, saying, "I am the light of the world. Whoever follows me will not walk in darkness, but will have the light of life."*

John 9:5 (NLT) *But while I am here in the world, I am the light of the world.*

Because Jesus brought light into the darkness of our world, we can live with the peace of God every day. When we follow the light that illumines the path God has for us, we can live more confidently, knowing that He guides us. How do we consistently follow that light? The answer is in Psalm 119:

Psalm 119:105 (NLT) *Your word is a lamp to guide my feet and a light for my path.*

Psalm 119:9-11 (AMP) *How can a young man keep his way pure? By keeping watch [on himself] according to*

Your word [conforming his life to Your precepts]. With all my heart I have sought You, [inquiring of You and longing for You]; Do not let me wander from Your commandments [neither through ignorance nor by willful disobedience]. Your word I have treasured and stored in my heart, That I may not sin against You.

We walk in peace when we have a relationship with Jesus, one of obedience and commitment to what He has shown us in His word. Once we surrender our lives to the Lord, we need to conscientiously walk with Him each day, moment by moment. A healthy relationship requires constant, consistent, intimate communication. God communicates with us through His word, and we are to respond honestly to God in prayer.

1 Thessalonians 5:17 (BLB) *Pray unceasingly.*

1 Thessalonians 5:17 (AMPC) *Be unceasing in prayer [praying perseveringly].*

"This is how you pray continually—not by offering prayer in words, but by joining yourself to God through your whole way of life, so that your life becomes one continuous and uninterrupted prayer."

Saint Basil the Great (48)

Is your peace within being disturbed? Satan has tried to disturb our peace and derail our writing as we have been writing about peace! We must always ask ourselves if we are maintaining the communication of our relationship with the Lord. When our peace is disrupted, do we remember to immediately refocus our eyes on Jesus, petition His help in prayer, and continue to live in His light and peace? Be intent and intentional in living at peace with God and at peace within yourself by keeping the line of communication open: studying and internalizing Scripture and persisting and persevering in prayer.

Father, we know the challenges we often face are the enemy of our souls trying to distract us from Your love, grace, mercy, and peace. Help us to focus in on Your truth and walk daily in Your peace.

Worship along with the Gaither Vocal Band as they sing "Chain Breaker" by Zach Williams: https://www.youtube.com/watch?v=8uDuHdoHNSA

FAITH LEADS TO PEACE

And Jesus told the woman, "Your faith has saved you; go in peace^{G1515}."

Luke 7:50

Each of the Gospel authors recount a story of Jesus being anointed by a woman, but they are not all about the same incident.

> All four gospels present an account of Jesus being anointed by a woman with a costly jar of perfume (Matthew 26:6–13; Mark 14:3–9; Luke 7:36–50; John 12:1–8). Matthew and Mark relate the same event but do not give the woman's name; Luke tells of a different woman, also anonymous, on an earlier occasion; and, in yet another event, the woman in John is identified as Mary of Bethany (John 11:2), sister to Martha and Lazarus. (49)

The occasion in the Gospel of Luke is a dinner at Simon the Pharisee's house. Apparently, Jesus was an invited guest. As the woman began washing Jesus's feet with her tears and anointing them with costly perfume, Simon wondered to himself whether Jesus could be a true prophet because, he reasoned, a prophet would have known what kind of woman she was and shunned her. However, he underestimated the Lord's ability to "know" about people because Jesus revealed that He knew what

Simon was thinking! He then pointed out Simon's failure to even treat Him as a guest by greeting Him with a kiss and having a servant wash His feet. Simon had not even fulfilled the reasonable expectations of hospitality during biblical times. However, the woman had continually kissed Jesus's dirty, smelly feet, washing them with her tears and drying them with her hair and then anointing them with the perfume. Jesus then puts Simon in the hot seat by telling a brief parable and asking Simon a question regarding it:

Luke 7:41-42 *"Two men were debtors to a certain moneylender. One owed him five hundred denarii, and the other fifty. When they were unable to repay him, he forgave both of them. Which one, then, will love him more?"*

Luke 7:43 *"I suppose the one who was forgiven more,"* Simon replied.

Jesus then revealed Simon's failures as a host and praised the woman's tender care of Him, tending to His needs after a journey by foot wearing sandals and anointing Him with perfume. He then said:

Luke 7:47 *". . . Therefore I tell you, her many sins have been forgiven, for she has loved much. But he who has been forgiven little loves little."*

When Jesus turns to the woman and tells her that her sins have been forgiven, the guests are all pondering what right He has to forgive sins. They may have been flabbergasted and incensed because they saw Him as a prophet but not yet as the Messiah. While they are all stuck in those thoughts, Jesus tells the woman, "Your faith has saved you. Go in peace."

Jesus knew the unnamed woman's heart. He knew her love for Him and that she realized her need of Him. She could "go in peace" because she now had peace with God because of her faith that Jesus was sent from God, and she received the forgiveness He offered. She could now embrace the result of that forgiveness which was peace with God, the peace of God, and peace with others as her life was being changed from the inside out.

We may not have had a "reputation" of sinfulness, but we have all been forgiven much. When sinfulness is defined as "falling short of the mark," we must all admit we miss the mark on a regular basis because the "mark" is sinless perfection. In God's economy there are no "little sins." All sin is an afront to a Holy God. The "little white lie", cheating on an exam or taxes, gossiping, are just as dire as murder. When we look at how much we have been forgiven, how strongly should we demonstrate our love for our Savior who died to pay the penalty of those sins. How can we express our love for Jesus today?

Father, we thank You for extending grace to us by sending Your Son to die in our place. We thank You that we can confess our sins daily and be forgiven and made new (1 John 1:9). We show our love for You in praise and worship but also in obeying Your command to love others and forgive them as You have forgiven us. Help us never to take that forgiveness lightly. Let us pour out our love in service to You!

Worship Experience: "Broken and Spilled Out" sung by Allison Durham Speer
https://www.youtube.com/watch?v=xUi3whcg8Ww

PARADE OF THE PRINCE OF PEACE

As He rode along, the people spread their cloaks on the road. And as He approached the descent from the Mount of Olives, the whole multitude of disciples began to praise God joyfully in a loud voice for all the miracles they had seen: "Blessed is the King who comes in the name of the Lord!" "Peace^{G1515} in heaven and glory in the highest!"

Luke 19:36-38

Psalm 118:26 *Blessed is he who comes in the name of the LORD. From the house of the LORD we bless you.*

The crowd lauded Jesus as King. They had the expectation that He would conquer the occupying Romans and set up an earthly kingdom immediately. They quoted from Psalm 118:26 which was widely accepted as a Messianic Psalm. The people were praising Jesus as the long-awaited Messiah who would bring peace. However, they did not understand the kind of peace He offered. The angel who announced the Messiah's arrival to the shepherds when Jesus was born proclaimed, "Glory to God in the highest, and on earth peace among those with whom he is pleased!" (Luke 2:14). The angel did not announce an absence of war or strife. He said there would be peace for those who trusted in God. As Jesus rode the colt in His coronation procession, He knew what the peace they were shouting about would cost

Him—His death on the cross—in a few short days. The One they thought would raise up an army to conquer Rome, would be nailed naked to a Roman cross and be raised up for the people to see His agony and shame. When they spoke of peace, they had no idea of its price. The peace Jesus purchased as the final, perfect sacrificial Lamb is the ability to be at peace with God and in an intimate Father/child relationship with the Creator of the universe!

Do you have this peace? It is offered to all who believe that Jesus is the Son of God, born of a virgin to live a sinless life on earth, who died on the cross to pay the penalty of our sin, and was raised from the grave three days later. Jesus now sits at the right-hand of God the Father in Heaven. You may have the peace and harmony with the Lord that Jesus died for by placing your trust in Him only, in Him alone.

Father, thank You for saving us by Your grace and giving us the faith to entrust our lives to Jesus. Thank you for the peace we enjoy even when life is creating all types of storms around us, the peace of knowing we are in Your hands, and You will never let us go.

John 10:27-30 *My sheep listen to My voice; I know them, and they follow Me. I give them eternal life, and they will never perish. No one can snatch them out of My hand. My Father who has given them to Me is greater than all. No one can snatch them out of My Father's hand. I and the Father are one."*

Worship along with Michael W. Smith's "Hosanna":
https://www.youtube.com/watch?v=C_E_5ScrnAY

IF ONLY YOU HAD KNOWN

As Jesus approached Jerusalem and saw the city, He wept over it and said, "If only you had known on this day what would bring you peace^{G1515}! But now it is hidden from your eyes. For the days will come upon you when your enemies will barricade you and surround you and hem you in on every side. They will level you to the ground—you and the children within your walls. They will not leave one stone on another, because you did not recognize the time of your visitation from God."

Luke 19:41-44

Jerusalem, the city of the Sanhedrin, the Pharisees, the leaders of the Jewish faith, should have been able to recognize Jesus as the Messiah based on the teachings of the Prophets. But they had blinded themselves to the truth that was right before their eyes. A very few of the religious leadership, such as Nicodemus and Joseph of Arimathea, saw Jesus for who He was—the Messiah, the Son of God, the One who would provide us the opportunity to be at peace with God. However, those who refused to see were, in the end, given over to their blindness by the Lord. They were looking only at the prophecies concerning the Messiah as conquering King and failed to see the truth that He came to bring peace with the Father—deliverance from sin, not deliverance from Rome. Jesus prophesied the judgment that would come upon Jerusalem for their failure to recognize Him as the Christ, the Son of God. Even though Jesus, the righteous judge, would eventually execute vengeance upon the city, He compassionately wept over them because of the judgement the Lord would have to carry out. Jesus shed tears for the very people who would shout "Crucify Him!", demanding His execution. Jesus, the Lamb of God, the perfect sacrifice, cried for those who would condemn Him to an agonizing and humiliating death on the cross. The events Jesus described would occur in AD 70 when the Romans besieged then demolished both Jerusalem and its inhabitants. The Temple and the city, including homes, were completely leveled. Most of the inhabitants were killed outright, and those who were not were taken prisoner to fight as gladiators or in other ways die as a spectacle for the Roman citizens. The reason for this future calamity upon Jerusalem was their failure to recognize Jesus. As the Voice translation says:

Luke 19:44b *because you did not recognize the day when God's Anointed One visited you.*

The Lord has revealed Himself in nature (Romans 1:20), through His Word, and through the testimony of believers. If you have not already seen the truth of Jesus, ask God to open your eyes. Seek Him in the Bible and listen to the witness of those who serve Him. Today is the day to recognize Jesus as the Son of the Living God and surrender your life to Him, the day of salvation is today, right now:

2 Corinthians 6:2 (NLT) *For God says, "At just the right time, I heard you. On the day of salvation, I helped*

you." Indeed, the "right time" is now. Today is the day of salvation.

Today, you can be at peace with God by trusting in the fact that Jesus, the Son of God, took your place on the cross and paid the debt for your sin. Jesus was the only acceptable substitutionary sacrifice for our sin because He lived a perfect, sinless life when He walked on earth as a man. He is the only path to true and lasting peace. Tomorrow is not promised to any of us. Trust in Jesus now!

Father, we thank You that we can be at peace with You rather than fearing Your righteous wrath because You placed our sin on Jesus who died to settle our debt. Then You imputed—transferred—Christ's righteousness to our account.

Worship with Conrad Fisher singing "He Paid a Debt": https://www.youtube.com/watch?v=nUYqoXhGjxw

PEACE BE WITH YOU

Then the two told what had happened on the road, and how they had recognized Jesus in the breaking of the bread. While they were describing these events, Jesus Himself stood among them and said, "Peace[G1515] be with you." But they were startled and frightened, thinking they had seen a spirit. "Why are you troubled," Jesus asked, "and why do doubts arise in your hearts? Look at My hands and My feet. It is I Myself. Touch Me and see—for a spirit does not have flesh and bones, as you see I have." And when He had said this, He showed them His hands and feet. While they were still in disbelief because of their joy and amazement, He asked them, "Do you have anything here to eat?" So they gave Him a piece of broiled fish, and He took it and ate it in front of them.

Luke 24:35-43

Suddenly, as Cleopas and his companion (some believe this could be Cleopas's wife) who had met Jesus on the road to Emmaus were recounting their experience, Jesus appeared in their midst. Jesus blessed them with, "Peace be with you." Peace is a word with many layers in the Greek:

> *eirḗnē*, i-ray'-nay; probably from a primary verb *eírō* (to join); peace (literally or figuratively); by implication, prosperity:—one, peace, quietness, rest, + set at one again. (50)

The disciples had been huddled inside with the door locked for fear that the Romans would arrest them as well. When Jesus said, "Peace be with you," they were in dire need of peace of mind. However, the peace Jesus offers is more than tranquility and calmness. It is to be "one" again, in other words, to be in right relationship with God which brings lasting peace. He offers us the opportunity to be in harmony with God instead of in discord.

It seems Jesus's words would have brought comfort to His followers. However, since He had just suddenly appeared in the middle of a locked room, they thought he was a ghost! Seriously, Disciples, weren't you all just talking about the fact the Jesus was alive and had appeared to Peter and now Cleopas and friend as well? Why would you think He wasn't real? Jesus patiently proved that He was indeed standing before them in the flesh by showing them the wounds in His hands and feet. They were amazed but still confused, so He asked for food and ate it in front them. He made the effort to bring them from frantic fear to perfect peace.

When Jesus calls us to follow Him, He offers us this peace with God, this wholeness that can only be found in a relationship with Him. We do not find this peace in following the rules or exercising certain religious rituals. To have this peace, we are required to be in an intimate relationship with our Savior and Lord, Jesus Christ. Surrendering our lives to Him and accepting the gift of salvation—freedom from the penalty of sin that He paid in our place once for all—is only the beginning. As we walk daily with Him by reading His word and living according to Scripture and taking every concern we have to God in prayer, we will experience the peace of God in our lives. Are you enjoying this peace on a daily basis? If not, first make sure you have a relationship with Jesus. Next, ask yourself if you are living in obedience to His commands. Then, be sure to pray. Talk to the Lord every day because He is your beloved friend.

Father, we thank You for sending Jesus to grant us peace with You through His death and resurrection. Help us to experience peace in our daily lives as we live for the pleasure of our First Love, Jesus. Remind us that there is no problem too difficult for You to solve, no need too great for You to provide, no sorrow too deep for You to comfort.

Worship along with Scott Wesley Brown singing "He will Carry You": https://www.youtube.com/watch?v=z-BCcBwnW1PU

LEGACY OF PEACE

Peace[G1515] *I leave with you; My peace*[G1515] *I give to you. I do not give to you as the world gives. Do not let your hearts be troubled; do not be afraid.*

John 14:27

Jesus gives us perfect peace. His peace is not dependent upon circumstances. We can have His peace in the middle of chaos because God is amazing, He's awesome, He's all-powerful. It is an all-consuming peace that envelopes the believer like a father's arms fold around a frightened child. Stuff is still going on, but the child feels safe in daddy's embrace. There is a famous painting titled "Peace in the Midst of the Storm" by Jack E. Dawson. There are several hidden images in it, but the best known is a perfect illustration of the peace that Jesus left as a legacy to all who would believe. In the middle of a violent storm with crashing waves, a white bird (dove?) has found quiet refuge in a cleft of the rocky cliff. The bird is completely undisturbed even though the tumult seems to be swirling around it.

The peace the Lord grants us is not an absence of trouble but confidence that God will see us through the storm. Jesus does not take away every uncomfortable or even painful experience, but He does enable us to be calm and peaceful not just after a trial but during it. Do you have this kind of peace? It is available to all who trust in

Jesus Christ, the Son of God, the Savior. It is evidence of the presence of the Holy Spirit within us.

Father, we thank You for Your peace that replaces our anxiety when we cast our cares on You.

Worship along with Guy Penrod singing "He Hideth My Soul":
https://www.youtube.com/watch?v=DUWXXEs-UqQ

PEACE DURING TRIBULATION

"Look, an hour is coming and has already come when you will be scattered, each to his own home, and you will leave Me all alone. Yet I am not alone, because the Father is with Me. I have told you these things so that in Me you may have peace^{G1515}. In the world you will have tribulation. But take courage; I have overcome the world!"

John 16:32-33

After following Jesus for three years, the disciples finally "got it" that Jesus was no mere man. He was sent directly from God. However, after their excited revelation, Jesus brought them back to the reality that they would flee in fear that very night; but He followed this prediction with a promise of peace.

> Jesus predicted the disciples would abandon Him, undoubtedly thinking of this as the fulfillment of Zechariah 13:7 (cf. Matt. 26:31; Mark 14:27). He said the "hour" was coming and indeed "has already come." At that moment, the mob gathered by Judas had already begun to light their torches. Soon, they would surround Gethsemane. (51)

Zechariah 13:7 *Awake, O sword, against My Shepherd, against the man who is My Companion, declares the LORD of Hosts. Strike the Shepherd, and the sheep will be scattered, and I will turn My hand against the little ones.*

Matthew 26:31 *Then Jesus said to them, "This very night you will all fall away on account of Me. For it is written: 'I will strike the Shepherd, and the sheep of the flock will be scattered.'*

Mark 14:27 *Then Jesus said to them, "You will all fall away, for it is written: 'I will strike the Shepherd, and the sheep will be scattered.'*

We know the rest of the story. Judas led the soldiers to the garden and identified Jesus by kissing Him on the cheek. Peter cut off the ear of one of the High Priest's servants, but Jesus healed the man. After Jesus was bound and taken from them, the disciples high-tailed it in different directions. How did these frightened, scattered sheep become the bold ambassadors of the Gospel? The peace Jesus promised them came after the resurrected Jesus appeared to them as they were gathered, huddled in fear that they, too, would be arrested. Having seen Jesus die on the cross and then appear before them, not as a spirit, but as a man they could touch and who could eat with them, they were convinced that He was the Messiah. However, their true boldness came after the Holy Spirit entered them in the upper room at Pentecost. That same Holy Spirit is who enables us to have peace in the middle of difficult circumstances and stand boldly for Jesus even when persecuted.

Jesus further promised that "in Him" we may have peace. This peace is not only peace with God (Rom. 5:1), but the subjective kind as well. Despite the chaos of living in a hostile world, we may experience tranquility. However, this too is conditional. Like joy, peace is available, but we must choose it. We choose peace when we choose to believe that Christ has "overcome" the world. (52)

16:33 Regardless of how the world beats you down, you have reason to live with bold faith because Jesus is the sovereign King over the world. He has defeated sin, Satan, and death. If you're a believer, your eternity is secure. And Jesus has the power to overrule your earthly circumstances. Knowing this truth and maintaining an intimate relationship with the Lord will radically change your perspective as you face whatever obstacles come your way. (53)

Are you able to be calm, to have peace, even when life seems to be throwing you curve ball after curve ball? Are you able to stand still and see how the Lord will work these situations for your good and His glory? Or are you still frantically panicking when the storm rages? Do you believe that Jesus has overcome the world? I (Susie) am sometimes a panicky person, especially when it comes to financial troubles or a loved one's medical crises. I have to remind myself to take a deep breath and pray to the One who can restore my peace. I have to remind myself that Jesus is Lord of all, everything I experience in this world is temporary, and ultimately all is well because Jesus has overcome the world. When the times of trouble come, and they will come, reflect on this statement, "But take courage; I have overcome the world!" When the storms of life rage against us, we must remember that even though we are not sure how all the pieces fit together, God is working all things for our good and His glory whether it feels like it at the time or not.

Father, thank You that because of Your mercy, grace, and power, we can have peace when everything around us seems to be falling apart. When we feel alone in our battle, help us to remember that You are with us always. We need to stand firm in our faith rather than feebly in our feelings. We need to be still and know that You are God.

Worship opportunities: Tennessee Ernie Ford singing "Stand by Me": https://www.youtube.com/watch?v=-c6axoy_MPj4

CeCe Winans singing "Never Lost": https://www.youtube.com/watch?v=Cl8EzTovAcs

SENT OUT WITH PEACE

It was the first day of the week, and that very evening, while the disciples were together with the doors locked for fear of the Jews, Jesus came and stood among them. "Peace[G1515] be with you!" He said to them. After He had said this, He showed them His hands and His side. The disciples rejoiced when they saw the Lord. Again Jesus said to them, "Peace[G1515] be with you. As the Father has sent Me, so also I am sending you.!"

John 20:19-21

The disciples, minus Judas the betrayer and Thomas who was absent from the meeting, were gathered together with the doors locked because they feared the Jewish leaders would have them arrested for following Jesus. Suddenly, Jesus inexplicably appeared in the middle of the room. Chuck Swindoll has an interesting observation about the difference between Jesus's resurrected body and that of Lazarus whom He had raised from the dead:

John includes this detail to illustrate for the first time in his narrative the different nature of Christ's resurrected body. Lazarus had been revived from death and restored to good health, but he lived with the same limitations, suffered illness and injury, and eventually died again. The resurrection of Jesus was fundamentally and profoundly different. It was, in fact, superior. His resurrection body, while still completely human, possessed supernatural qualities. He was raised to a new kind of life, never to die again. (54)

Luke tells us that, at first, the disciples thought Jesus might be a ghost. After all, He had just miraculously appeared in the middle of the room without walking through the door. One of our Sunday school teachers, Jerry Hines, believes that in our resurrected bodies, we will be able to travel at the speed of thought! However, after Jesus said, "Peace be with you," and showed them the scars in His hands and feet and even ate in front of them, they knew they were seeing Jesus in His resurrected body. Once they joyfully realized that it was truly Him, Jesus once again pronounced His blessing on them with "Peace be with you." Jesus then tells them that He is sending them out just as the Father had sent Him to them. Throughout His ministry, Jesus proclaimed that He only said what the Father had told Him and did what the Father had Him do. He then tells the disciples, "As the Father has sent me, so I am sending you." How can they have peace when the threat of arrest and possibly even crucifixion looms over their heads? How can they be sent out when persecution is eminent? Jesus is sending His disciples out to go where God leads them and do what God shows them in the power Jesus gives them. What power is this? Verse 22 makes it clear:

John 20:22 *When He had said this, He breathed on them and said, "Receive the Holy Spirit."*

This verse holds the key. Just as God breathed life into the first man, Jesus now breathes the Holy Spirit into His followers. He is sending them out not in their own power but with His power infused in them. When we place our trust in Jesus, surrendering our will to His, the Holy Spirit comes to reside in us. The Holy Spirit is the one who empowers us not only to remain at peace but to have the power to manifest all of the Fruit of the Spirit. We are sent out to be a "light" to the world. That light shines brightest when we are more and more like Jesus, when we are exhibiting the Fruit of the Spirit in our lives.

Are we going out into the world intentionally as Christ's instruments to proclaim the Gospel, the Good News that we can be at peace with God and have the peace of God? Are we secure in the peace that Jesus has given us, knowing that when He sends us out, He empowers us to do what He calls us to do?

Father, You have instructed us to go into all the world and make disciples (Matthew 18:18-20). By the power of Your Holy Spirit within us, help us to go boldly, being confident that Your peace is always available to us because You are with us always.

PEACE FOR THE DOUBTER

Eight days later, His disciples were once again inside with the doors locked, and Thomas was with them. Jesus came and stood among them and said, "Peace[G1515] be with you." Then Jesus said to Thomas, "Put your finger here and look at My hands. Reach out your hand and put it into My side. Stop doubting and believe."

Thomas replied, "My Lord and my God!"

Jesus said to him, "Because you have seen Me, you have believed; blessed are those who have not seen and yet have believed."

John 20:26-29

Thomas had not been present when Jesus suddenly appeared in the middle of the locked room before. Jesus again begins with "Peace be with you" addressed to all there, but perhaps especially for Thomas. Thomas was still not sure that Jesus had literally risen from the dead. In order for Thomas to be certain, Jesus offered him the opportunity to touch the wounds He suffered when crucified. At that point Thomas exclaimed, "My Lord and my God!" Thomas could now experience peace—wholeness, nothing broken and nothing missing, completeness. This peace is available to us as well. In fact, Jesus promised a blessing for those of us who have believed Him without being able to see Him in person as Thomas did. This kind of peace is only made possible through trusting Jesus as the Son of God who died as a sacrifice for OUR sin and was miraculously raised from the dead. Jesus Christ was the perfect, spotless, sinless Lamb of God. God in the person of the Son was His own Lamb.

Hebrews 7:27(NIV) *Unlike the other high priests, he does not need to offer sacrifices day after day, first for his own sins, and then for the sins of the people. He sacrificed for their sins once for all when he offered himself.*

Peace was available not only to Thomas and the other disciples of Jesus but for all who believe and place their trust in Jesus. Peace with God—freedom from the prison of our sin and the fear of God's wrath—is available through Jesus only. Once we have been given this gift by the grace of God, we can have peace within—peace during times of difficulty, peace when everything seems topsy turvy. We access this peace by internalizing Scripture and praying when tempted to worry. Make a list of Bible verses that remind you to be at peace. Perhaps a list of Scriptural songs that bring you peace would be useful as well. Perhaps you might write out your own "Prayer for Peace."

Father, in times of stress, illness, fear, remind us to bring it all to You with thanksgiving for the times You have helped us before and the knowledge that You will never leave us or fail us. Help us to peacefully rest de-

spite difficult circumstances as we lean in to be enveloped by Your presence.

Worship and allow yourself to be surrounded by His peace as you listen to The Martins singing "In the Presence of Jehovah"
https://www.youtube.com/watch?v=KNOjEeZsxXg

RESPITE TO REFUEL
AND REFINE

Then the church throughout Judea, Galilee, and Sa-maria experienced a time of peace^{G1515}. It grew in strength and numbers, living in the fear of the Lord and the encouragement of the Holy Spirit.

Acts 9:31

The author of Acts, Luke, had given a brief account of Saul's conversion in the beginning of Acts chapter nine. The word translated "Then" in this translation and "So" in others can also mean "Meanwhile." In other words, Luke is transitioning from the saga of Saul to what had been happening in the church at this time. The church was flourishing during a period of rest. They were using the break from constant persecution to grow in their knowledge and relationship with the Lord as well as in numbers of members.

9:31 It was a time of "peace" for the churches, but not a time of complacency, for they grew both spiritually and numerically. They seized the opportunity to repair and strengthen their sails before the next storm began to blow! (55)

9:31 the churches . . . had peace and were edified. Paul's conversion and political changes contrib-uted to the rest. A stricter Roman governor and

the expansion of Herod Agrippa's authority re-
stricted the persecution. (56)

When we have come through a tumultuous time of trial
and testing, and we are enjoying a break from the battles, it is tempting to fall back and just give in to lethar-
gy. The period of peace needs to be used to its fullest to
build ourselves up in the Lord. It is a time of preparation for the next storm or battle that is certain to come.
During times of relative calm, we need to use our time
wisely to study Scripture, take time for praise and worship of the God who brought us through the turmoil,
make efforts to build relationships within the community of faith, and pray for the strength to be victorious
when new problems arise. We cannot wait until we are
drowning to learn how to swim! We must become stronger disciples in preparation for future battles. Soldiers
go through boot camp but also training exercises during
times of peace. The army does not just lie around on their
cots until the next battle. We must remain prepared for
spiritual warfare. When we are receiving respite from
our own struggles, we also have the opportunity and the
energy to serve the Lord by serving others. We are to
mimic our Lord on this earth:

Matthew 20:28 (NLT) *For even the Son of Man came
not to be served but to serve others and to give his life
as a ransom for many.*

Are you up against a struggle right now? Use what you know of the Lord to give you strength. Look up Scripture. Pray. Seek out other believers to come alongside you. Are you in a time of peace? Strengthen yourself as a disciple of Christ by studying and internalizing His word, praying, fellowshipping, and worshipping. Be sure you are well-trained before the next battle comes your way.

Father, in our times of respite, make us stronger. Help us to use the time wisely to deepen our relationship with You and our knowledge of Your word which is our sword!

Worship with The Collingsworth Family singing "Praise the Lord":
https://www.youtube.com/watch?v=6iYC55-469U

PETER PROCLAIMS GOSPEL OF PEACE TO GENTILES

Then Peter began to speak: "I now truly understand that God does not show favoritism, but welcomes those from every nation who fear Him and do what is right. He has sent this message to the people of Israel, proclaiming the gospel of peace[G1515] *through Jesus Christ, who is Lord of all.*

Acts 10:34-36

Peter undoubtedly accepted the scriptural doctrine that God shows no partiality (see Deut. 10:17; 2 Chr. 19:7), but only in theory; only recently had he taken the doctrine seriously enough to act upon it. Either way, it's a transparent admission. He stood in the Gentile home because he himself had changed. (57)

Deuteronomy 10:17 *For the LORD your God is God of gods and Lord of lords, the great, mighty, and awesome God, showing no partiality and accepting no bribe.*

2 Chronicles 19:7 *And now, may the fear of the LORD be upon you. Be careful what you do, for with the LORD our God there is no injustice or partiality or bribery.*

Cornelius, a Roman centurion, was not a convert to Judaism but was what the Jews called a God-fearer. He gave generously to charity and prayed to the one true

God. However, He had not heard about the death, burial, and resurrection of Jesus Christ. An angel appeared, praising Him for his good deeds but urging him to send to Joppa to find Simon Peter who was staying in a house owned by Simon the tanner. Meanwhile, the Lord gave Peter a vision of unclean animals lowered down to him on a sheet. God instructed him to kill and eat. Peter replied that he had never eaten anything that had been declared "unclean". God replied, "Do not call anything impure that God has made clean" (Acts 10:15). The vision was repeated three times. Just as Peter was pondering what this could possibly mean, the men Cornelius had sent to find Peter arrived. The Lord instructed Peter to go with the men, so he invited them in and journeyed with them the next day. They arrived at the house of Cornelius.

Acts 10:27-28 *As Peter talked with him, he went inside and found many people gathered together. He said to them, "You know how unlawful it is for a Jew to associate with a foreigner or visit him. But God has shown me that I should not call any man impure or unclean."*

Cornelius invited Peter in to tell all his relatives and close friends whatever God had instructed him to share. If this were a cartoon version of the story, a lightbulb would suddenly appear above Peter's head. He now understood that the Gentiles should be given the same opportunity to hear the Gospel of Jesus Christ as the Jews. He shared the good news that peace with God can only be found by believing in and trusting in Jesus Christ. He realized the vision was to show him that all nations needed to hear the Gospel and all people could receive the forgiveness offered by the Lord.

We, too, are to share the good news of salvation by grace through faith in Jesus with all kinds of people—all nationalities, all races, all socio-economic groups, all abilities, etc. We cannot discriminate when it comes to telling others how to have peace with God. The great commission makes this clear:

Matthew 28:18-20 *Then Jesus came to them and said, "All authority in heaven and on earth has been given to Me. Therefore go and make disciples of all nations, baptizing them in the name of the Father and of the Son and of the Holy Spirit, and teaching them to obey all that I have commanded you. And surely I am with you always, even to the end of the age."*

Father, help us to faithfully proclaim the good news that anyone who believes in and places his/her trust in Jesus will have peace with You. We are not to judge who is worthy to hear. We are to proclaim the truth to everyone and trust You to draw them to You. Help our daily lives as well as our words to lead others to know You.

Worship along with Phillips, Craig, and Dean as they ask, "Can I Get a Witness?" Be encouraged to share your witness!

https://www.youtube.com/watch?v=f-q1qzOo4iw

GRACE AND PEACE
TO BELIEVERS IN ROME

To all in Rome who are loved by God and called to be
saints: Grace and peace[G1515] *to you from God our Father*
and the Lord Jesus Christ.

Romans 1:7

Paul's full salutation in this letter takes up the first seven verses of chapter one and is one extremely long sentence! I taught English, but do not ask me to diagram this sentence! First, Paul presents his credentials. Next, he articulates the Gospel in a nutshell. Then he addresses to whom he is writing. Paul had not yet been to Rome in person but is writing to believers in Rome. It is not known exactly how the church in Rome began, but it may be that visitors from Rome were in Jerusalem and heard Peter preach at Pentecost after the Holy Spirit fell in power upon approximately 120 men and women gathered in an upper room. These visitors could have returned to Rome and spread the Good News to others, both Jews and Gentiles. Note that he addresses these believers as "loved of God" and "saints." The word for "saint" derives from the word for "holy" and indicates they have been set aside to be purified for God's use. They did not perform a certain number of "good deeds" to become saints. God drew them to Himself, forgave their sin, and purified them by the blood of Jesus Christ shed in their place, the soap of God's love. On the cross, Jesus took on our sin and paid the price for it. Then He

PEACE: the Power of God's Presence

credited His righteousness to our account. All who have placed their trust in Jesus and yielded their will to His are saints. Therefore, Paul addressed his letter to the Christians in Rome, those who were believers in Jesus, the Messiah. We will let Charles Swindoll unpack the greeting Paul used:

"The double blessing of grace and peace was a signature greeting for Paul. "Grace" was a common greeting in Greek culture, and its inclusion here would have been as normal to his readers as is the greeting "Dear _____" to us today. However, Paul will delve into the deep theological significance of "grace" in his letter to the Romans in ways that no Jew or Greek would have expected. The Jews customarily greeted one another with shalom, which had the general meaning of "completion and fulfillment—of entering into a state of wholeness and unity, a restored relationship." The word embodied all the blessings of the Promised Land and the fulfillment of God's covenant with Abraham." (58)

When we surrender our lives to Christ, we leave behind the cruel master of our sin to join ourselves to the most Benevolent Master who adopts us into His family as a son or daughter. We become at peace with God because Jesus took the penalty of our sin on Himself on the cross and God now sees us as righteous. Our relationship with God that was marred by our sin is now completely restored, and we are in unity with Him. That peace with God then results in the peace of God, a state of well-being even in the middle of the chaos of this world. That is the greeting Paul bestowed on the Christians in Rome whom he had never met.

We must ask ourselves what we desire for our brothers and sisters in Christ. Do we hope for their peace? Do we pray for their peace as well as our own? Do we confer grace and peace upon other believers even when we may not agree with them on all points?

Father, help us to be avenues of peace within Your family. Help us to encourage others and remind them that peace is found in a right relationship with You. Please restore our peace when circumstances would steal it. Remind us that we are whole in You!

THE PEACE OF CHRIST
IS INCLUSIVE, NOT EXCLUSIVE

There will be trouble and distress for every human be-ing who does evil, first for the Jew, then for the Greek; but glory^{G1391}, honor^{G5902}, and peace^{G1515} for everyone who does good, first for the Jew, then for the Greek. For God does not show favoritism.

Romans 2:9-11

2:10 The verdict will be glory, honor, and peace to everyone, Jew or Gentile, who works what is good. And let us not forget that no one can work good, as far as God is concerned, unless he has first placed his faith and trust in the Lord Jesus Christ. The expression to the Jew first, and also to the Greek cannot indicate favoritism, because the next verse points out that God's judgment is impartial. So the expression must indicate the historical order in which the gospel went out, as in 1:16. It was proclaimed first to Jews, and the first believers were Jews. (59)

These verses emphasize that Jesus does not exclude people from being eligible to enter the Kingdom of God. Jesus taught mostly in Jewish gatherings, but do not forget that He also shared the Good News with the Samaritan woman who then evangelized her entire town who came out to listen to this man called Jesus in per-son. He ministered among them for two days.

John 4:39-41 *Many Samaritans from the village believed in Jesus because the woman had said, "He told me everything I ever did!" When they came out to see him, they begged him to stay in their village. So he stayed for two days, long enough for many more to hear his message and believe.*

This inclusiveness extends not only to Jew and Gentile but to all kinds of people—rich or poor, male or female, genius or "slow," able-bodied or "bed-found".

Galatians 3:28 (NASB) *There is neither Jew nor Greek, there is neither slave nor free, there is neither male nor female; for you are all one in Christ Jesus.*

As the *Believer's Bible Commentary* pointed out above. There is reward for anyone who "does good," but we must understand that in order to do what pleases God, we must believe, trust, rely on Jesus for salvation. Those who are "in Christ" will do the good works God has planned for them:

Ephesians 2:8-9 *For by grace you have been saved through faith; and that not of yourselves, it is the gift of God; not as a result of works, so that no one may boast. For we are His workmanship, created in Christ Jesus for good works, which God prepared beforehand so that we would walk in them.*

Therefore, those who have surrendered their lives to Jesus, will be rewarded with glory, honor, and peace. We have defined peace previously as a state of wholeness and reconciliation with God. We can relax peacefully when we have peace with God. We asked each other what exactly was meant by "glory" and "honor". We have included the portion of the definition of each that applies in this instance:

G1391 *dóxa* (D) Of that exalted state of blissful perfection which is the portion of those who dwell with God in heaven. As spoken of Christ and including the idea of His royal majesty as Messiah (Luke 24:26; John 17:5, 22, 24; 2 Thess. 2:14; 2 Tim. 3:16; 1 Pet. 1:11); of glorified saints, i.e., salvation, eternal life (Rom. 2:7, 10; 8:18; 1 Cor. 2:7; 2 Cor. 4:17; 1 Thess. 2:12; 2 Tim. 2:10; Heb. 2:10; 1 Pet. 5:1). (60)

G5902 *timế*, tee-may'; Of a state or condition of honor, rank, dignity, joined with dóxa (1391), glory (Heb. 2:7 quoted from Ps. 8:6); as conferred in reward (Rom. 2:7, 10; Heb. 2:9; 1 Pet. 1:7; 2:7). An office of honor (Heb. 5:4); glory and honor (Rev. 21:24, 26). (61)

When we join the Lord either by death or when He comes again, our bodies will be glorified, and we will be perfect. Here on earth, we bring glory to God by obedience and exhibiting the Fruit of the Spirit but cannot reach sinless perfection until we see Jesus face to face. God sees us as we will be because to Him it is already a reality. He sees glory in us through the Holy Spirit within us. "Honor" is not something we have earned by doing more good deeds than our neighbor. Honor is conferred on us by God because we are His children. These gifts of glory, honor, and peace are freely given to all who recognize Jesus as the Son of God and trust that His sacrifice on the cross was the only way we could be made right with God.

In the contrast described in Romans 2:9-11, which type of person are you? Are you the non-believer who does evil and will justly receive trouble and distress or are you trusting in Jesus who enables you to do good? If you are not sure whether you have a right relationship with Holy, Almighty God, let us help you nail that down right now. You can go to "Jewels of Salvation" in the back of this book to see what Scripture says about trusting Jesus. Or you could talk to a Bible teaching pastor or Sunday school teacher or reach out to us on our website www.preciousjewelsministries.com. We would love to show you how you can receive glory, honor, and peace through Jesus!

Father, our prayer is that all who read these devotional books will be drawn closer to You, either for the first time to become a new believer (brother or sister in Christ) or to become closer to You through daily exploring Your word, the Bible.

Worship opportunity: "In Christ, There is No East or West":
https://www.youtube.com/watch?v=S8xDtj2nGfs

THROUGH GOD'S GRACE,
I STAND IN PEACE

Therefore, since we have been justified through faith, we have peace^G1515 with God through our Lord Jesus Christ, through whom we have gained access by faith into this grace in which we stand. And we rejoice in the hope of the glory of God. Not only that, but we also rejoice in our sufferings, because we know that suffering produces perseverance; perseverance, character; and character, hope. And hope does not disappoint us, because God has poured out His love into our hearts through the Holy Spirit, whom He has given us.

Romans 5:1-5

We are justified through faith. What does that mean? The easiest explanation to remember is that God sees me "Just as if I'd" never sinned. Because of our relationship with Jesus by grace, through faith, we are at peace with God. This does not mean, however, that our lives will be free of trouble, strife, or even persecution. In fact, Jesus told His followers that we will have trouble:

John 16:33 *"I have told you these things so that in Me you may have peace. In the world you will have tribulation. But take courage; I have overcome the world!"*

Jesus indicated that despite the trouble we face, we can have peace! Paul writes of "this grace in which we stand."

Paul knew what standing in grace meant. He realized that only through grace could he enter the kingdom of heaven. He experienced the grace that enabled him to continue preaching the gospel after being beaten, ship-wrecked, and nearly stoned to death. Grace gave him the courage to stand firm in his faith when he was too weak to stand on his own two feet. Paul had a clear understanding of grace. Martyrs throughout history have understood the concept of standing in grace. Entering an arena to be torn apart by wild beasts is not something you face in your own strength. Continuing to pray for your persecutors as they are lighting the fire beneath you at the stake is only possible through grace. Thanking your pastor for teaching you about the Lord when he is pointing the executioner's gun at your breast in order to avoid his own execution is definite evidence of grace. (Read these and more examples in *The New Foxe's Book of Martyrs* rewritten and updated by Harold J. Chadwick.) These people and many persecuted Christians around the world today understand very well the grace in which they stand and the peace through which they overcome. The question is: do we? Do you and I have a clue what standing in God's grace is and what it can do in our lives? I hope so, because that grace is our power to live to the glory of God the Father. We are saved by grace. We live by grace. We must walk in grace. And we must stand firm in God's grace if we want to enjoy His peace.

Father, lead us to a deeper understanding of Your grace. Enable us to stand firm in the confidence of our

salvation and Your total control. We surrender our-
selves to You and trust You to hold us up by Your grace,
to bring the peace of Christ to our hearts to reside and
abide even when our world seems upside-down.

Be encouraged by listening to "I Will Go On" by Wes Hampton and the Gaither Vocal Band: https://www. youtube.com/watch?v=VzD7d0GnEHw&list=RDVzD-7d0GnEHw&start_radio=1

THE MIND OF THE SPIRIT
IS LIFE AND PEACE

Those who live according to the flesh set their minds on the things of the flesh; but those who live according to the Spirit set their minds on the things of the Spirit. The mind of the flesh is death, but the mind of the Spirit is life and peace[G1515]*, because the mind of the flesh is hostile to God: It does not submit to God's law, nor can it do so. Those controlled by the flesh cannot please God. You, however, are controlled not by the flesh, but by the Spirit, if the Spirit of God lives in you. And if anyone does not have the Spirit of Christ, he does not belong to Christ. But if Christ is in you, your body is dead because of sin, yet your spirit is alive because of righteousness. And if the Spirit of Him who raised Jesus from the dead is living in you, He who raised Christ Jesus from the dead will also give life to your mortal bodies through His Spirit, who lives in you.*

Romans 8:5-10

Paul contrasts having the "mind of the flesh" and the "mind of the Spirit." What does he mean? Having the mind of the flesh means being driven by our human desires, giving in to temptation and continuing to sin. A person who has truly been transformed by knowing and submitting to Jesus cannot remain in sin without feeling conviction—that nudge in the mind that lets a person know they need to confess their wrongdoing and ask the Lord to forgive them (1 John 1:9). Someone continuing in habitual sin probably has not been freed from slavery to sin by trusting in Jesus. That person is dead to the influence of the Holy Spirit because that Spirit does not live in him/her. A non-believer may think they are living it up, but in reality, they are plunging deeper and deeper toward eternal death—separation from God and all that is good. In contrast, those who have the mind of the Spirit are those who have put their trust in Jesus alone, knowing they could never be good enough to measure up to God's standards on their own. Once a person accepts God's gracious gift of salvation, His Holy Spirit comes to live in them. Their minds are now subject to the Spirit's influence. When we are committed and submitted to the leading of the Holy Spirit, we experience truly abundant life and peace within. J. Vernon McGee explains this well. He calls the mind of the flesh "carnally minded."

For to be carnally minded is death; but to be spiritually minded is life and peace [Rom. 8:6 KJV].

> "For to be carnally minded" means that you are separated from fellowship with God and that flesh is death here and now. The Spirit who indwells the believer brings life and peace. When we sin, we are to come to Him in confession and let Him wash us. This restores us to fellowship. The "life" He offers speaks of full satisfaction and the exercise of one's total abilities. Oh, to live life at its fullest and best! Many people think they are really living today, but it is a shoddy substitute

for the life God wants to provide. "Peace" means the experience of tranquility and well-being regarding the present and future. Oh, my beloved, how you and I need to get into that territory! (62)

Romans 8:10 (VOICE) *If the Anointed One lives within you, even though the body is as good as dead because of the effects of sin, the Spirit is infusing you with life now that you are right with God.*

Jesus promised that He came to give us life, and life more abundantly (John 10:10), or as The Voice translation reads: "life with joy and abundance." The passage we have examined today adds "peace" to what our relationship with Jesus brings us. We can truly live with joy and abundance when we reside calmly in the peace of God! Are you living peacefully, joyfully, and abundantly? If not, talk to the Lord about whatever is disturbing your peace and trust Him to restore it!

Father, as we've been studying peace, many trials have tried to disturb our peace and disrupt our writing schedule. Thank You for faithfully calming us down and getting us back on track. Thank You that the enemy was not able to rob us of our joy!!!

Worship along with "This I Believe (The Creed)" sung by Hillsong Worship, especially the chorus: https://www.youtube.com/watch?v=FtUNQpu2b7Q&list=RDFtUN-Qpu2b7Q&start_radio=1

OVERCOME EVIL WITH GOOD

Do not repay anyone evil for evil. Carefully consider what is right in the eyes of everybody. If it is possible on your part, live at peace[G1514] with everyone. Do not avenge yourselves, beloved, but leave room for God's wrath. For it is written: "Vengeance is Mine; I will repay, says the Lord." On the contrary, "If your enemy is hungry, feed him; if he is thirsty, give him a drink. For in so doing, you will heap burning coals on his head." Do not be overcome by evil, but overcome evil with good.

Romans 12:17-21

If possible, and to the extent that it depends on you, live in peace with all people.

Romans 12:18 (CJB)

G1514 *eirēneúō* (2) to cultivate or keep peace, i.e. harmony; to be at peace, live in peace. (63)

Insofar as it depends upon us, we are to live at peace with everyone (12:18). How? Paul suggested two responses, one passive and one active. First, when an enemy deliberately causes harm, we are to let it go unanswered . . . Here, Paul was referring to the deeds of an enemy—presumably someone outside the body of Christ, though not necessarily!—by which he or she clearly intends to harm another. Confrontation would be pointless. Paul's advice: Let it go . . . Paul's second suggested response is more active: Extend him or her the same hospitality you would a friendly stranger (12:20; quoting Prov. 25:21–22) . . . (64)

We live in a day of "road rage" and "going postal". A common attitude is, "I don't get mad; I get even!" However, we have already learned from Romans 12:2 that we are not to be like the world around us. According to the verses above, we should not try to even the score when we are wronged. We should remember the often quoted, "Two wrongs don't make a right," and continue to treat people the way we would have them treat us (Matthew 7:12). We are to make every effort to get along with others, even those who are difficult. We must trust God to deal with the evil around us and to administer discipline where it is needed. In fact, we are to extend hospitality even to our enemies, people we feel will never be our friends. We do good to extend the hospitality of food and drink to our friends when they are in need, but the Word says to do this for our enemies. Both here in Romans 12 and in Proverbs 25:21-22 we are told that being hospitable to our enemy will "heap burning coals on his head." We're not sure what all that entails, but we are sure it will help him or her to think about the way they've acted. The Proverbs passage goes on to say that "the Lord will reward you" for this kindness.

We conquer evil by continuing to do good. We subdue wrath with a soft answer (Proverbs 15:1). We prevail over our enemies with love and prayer (Matthew 5:43-44). We are victorious and are recognized as God's children when we strive to be peacemakers (Matthew 6:9). If we follow the scriptural prescription for dealing with those who would slander, malign, and intentionally try to harm us—evil doers or enemies, we will avoid the bitterness that comes with seeking retaliation. When we "let it go" unanswered or even do good to those who were determined to hurt us, it leaves room for God to convict them and maybe even extend grace to them and bring them into the "familyship." Our kindness may even lead them to repentance, not necessarily for the specific wrong done to us, but for their attitude. We need to save judgement for God but realize His discipline is used redemptively for their salvation. Only He knows what He is ultimately working in a person's life, and we dare not let our own anger get in His way.

Father, help us to stop and pray when we feel anger welling up inside us. Help us to trust You rather than to retaliate on our own when someone hurts us. Give us the strength to show kindness to those who would never show kindness to us. Help us to truly understand how to overcome evil with good.

Be not overcome by evil
but overcome evil with good.
No matter how bad someone hurts you,
Continue to act as you should.

PURSUE WHAT PROMOTES PEACE

For the kingdom of God is not a matter of eating and drinking, but of righteousness, peace^{G1515}*, and joy in the Holy Spirit. For whoever serves Christ in this way is pleasing to God and approved by men. So then, let us pursue*^{G1377} *what leads to peace*^{G1515} *and to mutual edification.*

Romans 14:17-19

In the beginning of Romans 14, Paul discusses the fact that some Christians were concerned that other believers were eating meat that had been sacrificed to idols. There was division in the church at Rome because of this.

While many things in the Christian life are essential, some are not. The two specific disputable matters that Paul addressed in Romans 14 were chiefly regarding which foods were acceptable to eat (verses 2–3) and the observance of certain holy days (verses 5–6). He also touched on drinking wine in verse 21. (65)

Paul says that he is convinced that nothing is "unclean" in and of itself, and believers have liberty to eat and drink all things. However, he also makes it clear that if a person is convicted that he should not eat or drink those items, it would be sin for him to do so. The person who has freedom to eat all things should not offend the one who abstains from them by flaunting his liberty. Neither should the one who abstains judge the one who eats and drinks. Those are side matters that do not have any bearing on a person's salvation which is entirely by grace through faith in Jesus Christ. We do not need to focus on the external observances but on the attitude of the heart. We need to be actively pursuing peace and unity with our brothers and sisters in Christ. Today, church members do not fret over food sacrificed to idols, but we have other external issues that we allow to divide us and disturb the peace of the body of Christ. Charles Swindoll had something to say about this:

> The essence of Christianity is not found in external matters (14:17–19). Jesus said, "It is not what enters into the mouth that defiles the man, but what proceeds out of the mouth, this defiles the man" (Matt. 15:11). How easy to get hung up on tangible things such as foods, habits, clothing, recreation, music, and even decorations. The organ of life's richest delights is not the stomach; it's the heart. At the end of the day we will answer not for what we put into our stomachs but for the attitudes we nurtured in our hearts. (66)

Is our attitude toward a brother or sister who dresses less conservatively than us one of judgement or acceptance? Are we aghast when a church member has an alcoholic beverage in public? It is not our job to bring conviction about matters that cannot rob us of our salvation. The

Holy Spirit does not need our help! Jesus is our Master, and as Paul said in verse 4, we each answer to Him, and it is only His right to judge. However, Paul also assures that we will stand and not fall because our Master is able to keep us standing. Our attitude must always be one of redemption. We must extend grace to others and relentlessly pursue, run after, be intent on nurturing peace within the church, the body of believers.

> G1377 *diōkō* To follow or press hard after, to pursue with earnestness and diligence in order to obtain, to go after with the desire of obtaining (Rom. 9:30, 31; 12:13; 14:19; 1 Cor. 14:1; Phil. 3:12, 14; 1 Thess. 5:15; 1 Tim. 6:11; 2 Tim. 2:22; Heb. 12:14; 1 Pet. 3:11) (67)

Tony Evans makes this point clearly in his study Bible:

> 14:19-21 The goal of the kingdom is not to keep other people in line with our preferences, but to pursue what promotes peace (14:19). We can use our freedom in two ways: either we tear down God's work (14:20) in people's lives by flaunting our liberty, or we build up one another (14:19) by being sensitive to our weaker brothers and sisters. The irony is that while we may have the freedom to do something, if we continue to do it knowing it will make our brother stumble, that action suddenly becomes evil. On the contrary, it is a good thing not to . . . do anything that makes

someone stumble, which means to trip them up
spiritually (14:21). (68)

We must be consistent in asking ourselves whether or
not exercising the freedom we have in Christ may harm
a brother or sister. Do we pursue peace? Do we work at
graciously building a brother or sister up in Christ rather than tearing them down for some non-essential matter? Our brotherly/sisterly love within the "familyship"
of God will help us to live at peace with one another.

Colossians 3:14 (AMP) *Beyond all these things put on
and wrap yourselves in [unselfish] love, which is the
perfect bond of unity [for everything is bound together
in agreement when each one seeks the best for others].*

*Father, help us to not judge others over external things.
Help our focus to be loving Your "familyship" and encouraging each other to grow in our knowledge of and
obedience to what Jesus commanded. He prayed for us
the night He was arrested that You would make us one.
Please help us to pursue peace and seek unity and harmony among believers.*

FILLED WITH JOY AND PEACE

Now may the God of hope fill you with all joy and peace[G1515] as you believe in Him, so that you may overflow with hope[G1680] by the power of the Holy Spirit.

Romans 15:13

In the beginning of Romans 15, Paul summed up the problem of the dispute in the church at Rome regarding eating food offered to idols or "unclean" food as described in the Old Testament Law and whether or not certain Jewish Holy days must be observed. He again makes the case that unity in the church is more important than these disputable matters. He urges them to accept one another. He reminds them, also, that the Gentiles were included in the promise to Abraham that through his Seed all nations would be blessed. Then Paul prays a blessing on all the believers at Rome in verse 13 above. In Charles Stanley's *Life Principles Bible*, he writes:

> The Christian life is to be characterized by hope, joy, and peace. As we grow in His grace, God wants us to experience each of them in increasing measure. If they're lacking, we know something has gone wrong. (69)

We have hope, the expectation of an eternity with God, because of Jesus and the Holy Spirit within us.

G1680. elpís; gen. elpídos, fem. noun. Hope, desire of some good with expectation of obtaining it . . . (II) Spoken especially of those who experience the hope of salvation through Christ, eternal life, and blessedness (Rom. 5:2, 4, 5; 12:12; 15:4, 13,) "the God of hope" means the author and source of hope, not the one who needs hope. (70)

15:13 God of hope. God is the source of eternal hope, life, and salvation, and He is the object of hope for every believer (see note on 5:2). by the power of the Holy Spirit. The believer's hope comes through the Scripture (cf. 15:4; Eph. 1:13, 14), which was written and is applied to every believing heart by the Holy Spirit. (71)

Our hope should result in joy, the abundance of life that Christ came to give us. Our joy should increase as we know Jesus more deeply through His word and the illumination of the Holy Spirit within us. We should also increase in peace. Not only the peace of God that assures us even in the midst of troubles but the peace with others that Paul has been urging the believers at Rome to cultivate.

We can live in harmony with other believers even if we do not agree on every point or practice. What can we do to promote this harmony within our local churches? Perhaps we need to judge less and listen more. Perhaps we need to set aside the "need" to be always "right" and just agree to disagree on some matters. If we agree on salvation by grace alone through Christ alone, much of the other stuff is minor. Let us focus on that which brings us together rather than anything that would seek to divide us.

Father, show us when we have been majoring on the minor things rather than celebrating the major things that unite us. Help us to be one in the unity of Your love. Prevent us from causing division in the local body of believers. Help us to truly be one in the Spirit.

Worship along with "They'll Know We are Christians by Our Love:"
https://www.youtube.com/watch?v=t-W5HEVP-JT8&list=RDt-W5HEVPJT8&start_radio=1

GOD OF PEACE

The God of peace^{G1515} be with all of you. Amen.

Romans 15:33

15:33 the God of peace. Just as He is the God of hope (see note on v. 13), God is also the source of true peace (cf. Eph. 2:11–14; Phil. 4:7). (72)

15:33 And now Paul closes the chapter with the prayer that the God who is the source of peace might be their portion. In chapter 15 the Lord has been named the God of patience and consolation (v. 5), the God of hope (v. 13), and now the God of peace. He is the source of everything good and of everything a poor sinner needs now and eternally. Amen. (73)

God is the source of all good things; and if we lack anything, we can ask Him.

John 14:13-14 *And I will do whatever you ask in My name, so that the Father may be glorified in the Son. If you ask Me for anything in My name, I will do it.*

To ask "in My name" isn't just to add "in Jesus's name" at the end of your petition for whatever you want. In His name means in keeping with His character, His Word, and His will.

1 John 5:14 *And this is the confidence that we have before Him: If we ask anything according to His will, He hears us.*

In accordance with His will would be in accordance with His word, the Holy Scripture. In addition, we do not choose verses like choosing a la carte in a restaurant. What we ask needs to be in keeping with the whole counsel of God. James uses the example of asking the Lord to give us wisdom:

James 1:5 *Now if any of you lacks wisdom, he should ask God, who gives generously to all without finding fault, and it will be given to him.*

God is the source of all good things, every perfect gift.

James 1:17 *Every good and perfect gift is from above, coming down from the Father of the heavenly lights, with whom there is no change or shifting shadow.*

Peace is one of the attributes listed in the Fruit of the Spirit. Therefore, we know it is consistent with God's word and will. Has your peace been disturbed lately by circumstances out of your control or even in a way that seems to be a direct attack from our enemy, Satan? You may confidently, boldly ask the Lord to restore your peace of mind, your tranquility, because He is the source of that peace. As soon as you realize that you are not at peace, lift up your prayer for peace while at the same time thanking God for the answer (Philippians 4:6-7).

Father, we thank You for answered prayer, especially in times of distress when it would be easy to fall into worry or even despair. We know that You work all things for our good and Your glory. Help us to live out that confidence every moment of every day by relaxing in Your peace.

Worship experience: "There is Peace on Earth" sung by Claire Ryan Crosby:
https://www.youtube.com/watch?v=Waitmz6C1oo

GOD OF PEACE TO CRUSH SATAN

The God of peace^{G1515} *will soon crush Satan under your feet. The grace of our Lord Jesus Christ be with you.*

Romans 16:20

Starting in Romans 16:17, Paul warns the members of the church in Rome to watch out for persons who try to cause a division among them. There will always be those who enjoy creating drama by pitting one group against another by causing arguments. There are also false teachers who stray from the truth of Scripture and mislead people. They are skilled at making their position sound good. Paul declares that they are not truly serving the Lord Jesus but their own "bellies" or "appetites." Paul rejoiced over the obedience of the Roman church but reminded them to be "wise about what is good and innocent about what is evil" (Romans 16:19). He was confident that the church at Rome would "crush Satan" under their feet by the power of the Holy Spirit. This reminds us of God's promise to Eve:

Genesis 3:15 (AMP) *And I will put enmity (open hostility) Between you and the woman, And between your seed (offspring) and her Seed; He shall [fatally] bruise your head, And you shall [only] bruise His heel.*

Through the power of the Holy Spirit in them, the members of the church at Rome would be able to discern truth, weed out those who would divide, and in so doing crush Satan's efforts.

Charles Swindoll gives us guidelines for identifying whether or not something is true:

> Here are four questions every member of a church should be trained to ask. Think of them as truth filters. Everything we hear should easily pass through all four.
>
> • "Does what I am hearing agree with Scripture?"
> • "Does what I am hearing honor my Lord and Savior, Jesus Christ?"
> • "Does what I am hearing help me become more godly?"
> • "Does what I am hearing cause me to think more highly of my fellow believers?" (74)

If we as church members would ask those four questions, we would not be quick to believe something that would create conflict in the body of Christ and destroy our unity and peace. God is the source of peace, not confusion or division. God desires all believers to be at peace with one another. May we all learn to ask those four questions to be able to spot anyone or anything that would cause us to be at odds with each other rather than at peace.

Father, may we always seek peace with others but never at the sacrifice of truth and integrity. Help us to examine whether or not a statement is in line with Scripture, honors Jesus, makes us more like Jesus, and makes us think highly of another believer. Help us to study and internalize Your word in order to apply it and use it to test teaching that we hear or read.

Sing along with Chris Tomlin singing "Romans 16:19": https://www.youtube.com/watch?v=VdsowUx-W8VE&list=RDVdsowUxW8VE&start_radio=1

TRENDING NOW: GRACE AND PEACE

Grace and peace to you from God our Father and the Lord Jesus Christ.

1 Cor. 1:3, 2 Cor. 1:2, Gal. 1:3, Eph.1:2, Phil. 1:2, 1 Thess. 1:1, 2 Thess. 1:2, Titus 1:4

What greeting do you use when you meet a long-time friend or write a letter to a loved one? Do you say, "Hi! How are you?" to which they reply the obligatory, "Fine. How are you?" Paul greeted the believers to whom he wrote by pronouncing "Grace and peace, from God the Father and the Lord Jesus Christ our Savior." You may be thinking that Paul could officially say that to Titus, Timothy, and others because he was an Apostle and writing scripture. However, can we not confidently say that God bestows grace and peace on all who trust in Jesus? Paul desired that his children in the faith understand the grace—the unmerited favor—of God more and more as they grew in their knowledge of Jesus. He reminded them of the peace, the wholeness, the contentment that was theirs through the indwelling Holy Spirit.

I wonder what would happen if we began greeting other Christians in this manner? I think it would feel extremely weird at first (I hope they would not call the people in the white coats); but, seriously, perhaps it would encourage someone to rest in the fact that he or she is a child of

God. Perhaps we would be encouraged to truly minister these gifts from God in our daily dealings with others. In our correspondence—okay, let's be real—in our emails, tweets, and Facebook posts, perhaps we could remind each other of the grace and peace that is ours through the Lord Jesus Christ. I am going to try it! Perhaps if you try it, too, we can start a trend.

Father, whether we use these exact words as a greeting or parting blessing or not, let us share Your grace and peace through our words, actions, and attitudes every day. Thank You for bestowing that grace and peace upon us.

Relax and listen to Fernando Ortego singing "Grace And Peace (2 Thessalonians 1:2)": https://www.youtube.com/watch?v=sqSc-6207JU&list=RDsqSc-6207JU&start_radio=1

PERFECT HARMONY: LIVE IN PEACE

Finally, brothers, rejoice! Aim for perfect harmony, encourage one another, be of one mind, live in peace[G1514]. *And the God of love and peace*[G1515] *will be with you.*

2 Corinthians 13:11

13:11-13 These exhortations apply to all believers: rejoice, become mature, be encouraged, be of the same mind, be at peace. We are capable of all these actions because of the work of God in our lives. If the Corinthians followed through, the God of love and peace would be with them and grant them his power (13:11). (75)

Live in peace. This was Paul's goal for all the churches—that they bear with one another without conflict. Sadly, neither the church in Corinth nor most churches throughout history, even into our own day, have completely modeled this. Yet we must all strive for peace in our relationships with fellow members of the body of Christ. (76)

Paul had written to the church at Corinth to admonish them to turn from false teachers and from Jewish teachers who were trying to put them back under the Law of Moses. There were also divisions within the church and blatant sin. Paul urges each person to examine him/herself as to whether they were truly in Christ in the sense of having received salvation but also in the sense of bearing evidence of the Holy Spirit working in their lives (i.e. the Fruit of the Spirit). He begins his closing remarks in verse 11 reminding them to rejoice, live in harmony, be encouraging to each other, be like-minded, and live peaceably with others in the church. They were to be in relentless, tenacious pursuit of peace in relationship with others as well as in relationship with God. God is the source of our love for each other and our ability to be at peace with each other. Live in harmony can be translated as restoration or reconciliation:

2 Corinthians 13:11 (VOICE) *Finally, brothers and sisters, keep rejoicing and repair whatever is broken. Encourage each other, think as one, and live at peace; and God, the Author of love and peace, will remain with you.*

Do you have any broken relationships with brothers or sisters in your local church? Do you feel there is discord rather than harmony with another church member? Remember what we learned in Romans 12:18, "If it is possible on your part, live at peace with everyone." Work to repair what is broken to be able to walk in harmony with others in the "familyship."

Father, help us to be in harmony with others. There must be unity in the church. We may each have our own areas of service and interest, and we may not always agree on exactly how to do something. We do not have to be in unison (all singing the same note), but we must harmonize (each singing different notes that go well together, complementary to one another). Help us never to be the ones to create discord but be known as peacemakers.

Worship along with the Gaither Vocal Band and the Oakridge Boys singing "That's Gospel, Brother": https://www.youtube.com/watch?v=5bGfMB9sONQ

FRUIT OF THE SPIRIT: PEACE

But the fruit of the Spirit is love, joy, peace^{G1515}, patience, kindness, goodness, faithfulness, gentleness, and self-control. Against such things there is no law.

Galatians 5:22-23

The characteristic of the fruit of the Spirit we are focusing on in this book is peace. Here are some basic facts about biblical peace from an article found online at https://loveinbible.com/how-many-times-is-peace-mentioned-in-the-bible/

- Peace is mentioned more than 300 times in the Bible, with the highest occurrence in the book of Isaiah.
- The Hebrew word for peace is "shalom" denoting completeness, soundness, and welfare.
- The Greek word for peace is "eiréné" emphasizing unity and rest.
- Peace in the Bible goes beyond the absence of conflict and encompasses restoration and inner tranquility.
- Jesus is the source of peace offering reconciliation with God, peace with others, and peace within ourselves. (77)

Peace with God, being reconciled to Him and freed from the chains of our sin because of His grace and Christ suffering the penalty for our sins, has to be the beginning place of peace. Once we have received the gift of salvation—peace with God—then we can begin experiencing and cultivating peace within ourselves by internalizing God's promises to us in Scripture. We will have access to the peace of God. Then we will be responsible to live at peace with others. As we are seeing, the Bible has much to say about the fact that we should make every effort to maintain peace with other people.

Have you secured peace with God through faith in Jesus? Are you experiencing tranquility in your day-to-day life because the Holy Spirit dwells in you bringing you peace? Do you find yourself more successful at having peace with others because of your walk with Jesus? We hope these pages will help you grow stronger in peace. Peace comes from the power of God's Holy Spirit within us.

Father, Your presence is powerful and gives us the power to remain calm in any storm of life. Being at peace within ourselves is a position of power because we are not easily ruffled. Help us to remember to tap into the power of Your peace! Help us to always be able to say, "It is well with my soul!"

Please take the time to listen to Hugh Bonneville narrate the story behind the hymn "It is Well with My Soul". https://www.youtube.com/watch?v=ReApJymYSiw

But now you have been united with Christ Jesus. Once you were far away from God, but now you have been brought near to him through the blood of Christ.

Ephesians 2:13 (NLT)

I WILL TESTIFY ABOUT HIS BLOOD

"Let's not talk about the blood," they say,
"That turns off the people of today."
But don't they know it's the only way
to know peace with God for which Jesus paid?

God sent Christ to die in our rightful place.
The blood that He shed provides God's grace
to save us from Hell to Heaven and God's face.
It covers our sin and leaves no trace.

If it had not been for the blood Jesus shed
from His hands, His feet, His side, His head:
if He had not died, then arose from the dead;
There would be no hope. There'd be only dread.

I'll think of His precious blood, and I'll sing.
I'll rejoice in Him and praises I'll bring.
To tell of His blood glorifies Christ the King.
To receive its power is a wonderful thing.

I'll thank the Lord that He died for me.
I'll tell others about Him and pray they will see
that the blood of the Lamb can set them free.
The blood brings the greatest joy there can be.

I'll continue to talk about His blood without shame.
I'll sing the Lord's praises for taking my blame.
He died in my place, and I'll never be the same.
I love Him and praise Him and glorify His name.

Join in worship with CeCe Winans and the Martins
singing "The Blood will Never Lose Its Power" by Andre
Crouch:
https://www.youtube.com/watch?v=wypnXMJnFoI

JESUS: THE SOURCE OF PEACE FOR ALL WHO TRUST HIM

Therefore remember that formerly you who are Gentiles in the flesh and called uncircumcised by the so-called circumcision (that done in the body by human hands)— remember that at that time you were separate from Christ, alienated from the commonwealth of Israel, and strangers to the covenants of the promise, without hope and without God in the world. But now in Christ Jesus you who once were far away have been brought near through the blood of Christ. For He Himself is our peace^{G1515}, who has made the two one and has torn down the dividing wall of hostility by abolishing in His flesh the law of commandments and decrees. He did this to create in Himself one new man out of the two, thus making peace^{G1515} and reconciling both of them to God in one body through the cross, by which He extinguished their hostility. He came and preached peace^{G1515} to you who were far away and peace to those who were near. For through Him we both have access to the Father by one Spirit.

Ephesians 2:11-18

There had long been a divide between the Jews and the Gentiles—anyone not of the nation or religion of the Jews. The Gentiles were "far off" as in not near to the one true God. God had promised Abraham that all nations would be blessed through him (Genesis 18:17-19); but rather than sharing God with the Gentiles, the

Jews had used the Law to alienate them. In the Complete Jewish Study Bible, Ephesians 2:17 is linked with Isaiah 57:19 indicating that Isaiah prophesied that the Messiah would extend peace to both Jew (those who are near) and Gentile (those who are far away).

Isaiah 57:19 (CJB) *I will create the right words: 'Shalom, Shalom to those far off and to those nearby!' says Adonai; 'I will heal them!'*

Ephesians 2:17 (CJB) *Also, when he came, he announced as Good News shalom to you far off and shalom to those nearby, news that through him we both have access in one Spirit to the Father.*

Jesus brought peace to both Jew and Gentile through His death on the cross. Peace with God is available to all kinds of people by grace through faith in Christ. Christ also brings peace between people of different backgrounds. Charles Swindoll summarizes this truth well:

> In short, when Jesus Christ paid the penalty for the sins of all humanity—Jews and Gentiles alike—the wall of separation crumbled. As Paul had written to the Galatians, "There is neither Jew nor Greek, there is neither slave nor free man, there is neither male nor female; for you are all one in Christ Jesus" (Gal. 3:28). Christ Himself—and Christ alone—is our peace (Eph. 2:14). The Greek text places a strong em-

phasis on "Himself," reminding us, as Paul has throughout this letter, that our new life has been given to us as a gracious gift provided by Christ's work alone. He has bestowed this gift upon us by grace alone through faith alone. What a glorious truth! Christ alone is peace personified. Centuries earlier, Isaiah prophesied that the promised child born of the family of David would be called "Prince of Peace" (Isa. 9:6). Through the baptism of the Holy Spirit, every believer shares a common union of peace with each other: whether Jew or Gentile; male or female; black, white, Asian, or Hispanic; rich or poor; educated or uneducated; strong or weak. The racial, ethnic, political, social, and economic dividers that cause so much conflict in our world fade into insignificance when the Son of God brings spiritual peace. (78)

In Christ, all people have the same spiritual standing: "There is neither Jew nor Gentile, neither slave nor free, nor is there male and female, for you are all one in Christ Jesus" (Galatians 3:28). Regardless of our race, gender, or nationality, we are all saved the same way, and, once saved, we are "fellow citizens" and members of God's household (Ephesians 2:19). Together in Jesus Christ, "the whole building is joined together and rises to become a holy temple in the Lord" (Ephesians 2:21). (79)

Paul's message to the church at Ephesus was not for the early church alone. It is as current today as it was in Paul's day. There are many things that divide people. However, for those in the body of Christ, those of us who have received the gift of salvation by grace alone through faith in Christ alone, there should be no divisions. We should be at peace with all others in what the Complete Jewish Bible calls the Messianic Community, those who have trusted in Jesus as the Messiah promised to the Jews.

Unity in the church was a frequent topic in Paul's writings. When a teacher wants to emphasize an important concept, he/she repeats that concept over and over in many different ways to drill it into the students. This tells us that the Lord inspired Paul to drill unity and peace within the church to his readers, including us today! Are we as believers living in peace with each other. Are we as individual believers living in peace with other individual believers as much as it depends on us? (Romans 12:18)

Father, help us to begin with an attitude of wanting to be at peace with others. Help us to be welcoming to brothers and sisters from all backgrounds, races, political parties, etc. because we are united by the blood of Jesus. You love us and call us as individuals, but Your blood also washes away all divisive lines. Lord, help us to truly be one in the Spirit. Jesus, You are the true source of our peace.

Worship with Wes Hampton and the Gaither Vocal Band singing "He is Here": https://www.youtube.com/watch?v=A97aLphdLoo

PRACTICE AND PRESERVE THE BOND OF PEACE

As a prisoner in the Lord, then, I urge you to walk in a manner worthy of the calling you have received: with all humility and gentleness, with patience, bearing with one another in love, and with diligence to preserve the unity of the Spirit through the bond of peace[G1515].

Ephesians 4:1-3

Paul reminded the Ephesians that he was in prison due to his mission ordained by the Lord to preach the gospel—the good news of salvation through Jesus Christ for all who believe—to the Gentiles. His imprisonment was in accordance with divine design. This would remind them that service to the Lord Jesus could come at a price to them as well. Paul admonished them to live a life worthy of their salvation and the specific gifts the Holy Spirit had bestowed on them. They should be worthily living out the purpose for which they were created. Not that they earned salvation in any way, but that their behavior would be evidence of the change brought about in them by the Holy Spirit.

Ephesians 4:2 *T*he apostle now specifies four graces that evidence this essential proportion between calling and character: humility, gentleness, patience, and forbearance. These are all qualities necessary for good relations with others in the Christian community and beyond. (80)

Believers should be consistently characterized by humility and patience toward others by the power of the Holy Spirit working within them. Overall, our interactions with other believers should be the result of love, the kind of love that can only come from a relationship with the Lord Jesus. The Fruit of Spirit as well as the attributes Paul just listed here all build one upon the other, but the foundation of all of them is Christ-like love.

> "Love" is a recurring theme in Ephesians. The four graces Paul recommends here are all aspects of love and are exemplified to perfection in Christ (Php 2:2, 5). (81)

The graces described in this verse and the love they exemplify can only be achieved when the Holy Spirit is flowing through believers as we present ourselves as instruments of God's purposes. We cannot do any of this in our own strength. In Christ, we can do all He calls us to do, but without Him, we are incapable of accomplishing His will. Our longsuffering and seeking peace are a direct result of the love the Holy Spirit gives us for our fellow (and sister) believers. We are to have a "bond of peace." What does this mean? We looked up bond and as a result of that, looked up "ligament":

> G4886 sýndesmos, soon'-des-mos; from G4862 and G1199; a joint tie, i.e. ligament, (figuratively) uniting principle, control:—band, bond. (82)

LIG'AMENT, noun [Latin ligamentum, from ligo, to bind, that is, to strain.]

1. Any thing that ties or unites one thing or part to another.

Interwoven is the love of liberty with every ligament of your hearts.

2. In anatomy, a strong, compact substance, serving to bind one bone to another. It is a white, solid inelastic, tendinous substance, softer than cartilage, but harder than membrane.

3. Bond; chain; that which binds or restrains. (83)

The bond of peace that holds us together as the body of Christ is like the ligaments that hold our bones together. When I had torn ligaments and tendons in my ankle, surgery was required to restore the stability of that joint. At this point in history, it seems that ligaments of Christ's body have been injured. There is a divide among the people of this country and even among believers. We must "endeavor" as the King James Version translates this verse, to return to the bond of peace that unites us. The New Testament word for peace relates to the Old Testament "shalom" which involves wholeness or as Susan has defined it "nothing missing, nothing broken." There is brokenness among Christians in America, and our sincere prayer is that the Holy Spirit will restore the bond of peace that unites us! Lord, help us be diligent to seek unity! Divisiveness in the church is harmful not only to those failing to come together in unity, but also harms those observing this behavior. This should never be! It grieves the heart of the Lord when we are divided. Jesus prayed for us to be united as one in His high priestly prayer.

John 17:20-21 *I am not asking on behalf of them alone, but also on behalf of those who will believe in Me through their message, that all of them may be one, as You, Father, are in Me, and I am in You. May they also be in Us, so that the world may believe that You sent Me.*

Father, Your desire is that we be one, united family in Jesus Christ. Help us to endeavor to bridge the gaps between each other. Help us to be united rather than fragmented. Let our unity be a witness to the world.

How should we walk? Listen to The Gaither Vocal Band united with Ernie Haase and Signature Sound singing "I Then Shall Live": https://www.youtube.com/watch?v=VNisXkfuo7k

BOOTS OF PEACE?

Therefore take up the full armor of God, so that when the day of evil comes, you will be able to stand your ground, and having done everything, to stand. Stand firm then, with the belt of truth buckled around your waist, with the breastplate of righteousness arrayed, and with your feet fitted with the readiness of the gospel of peace[G1515]. In addition to all this, take up the shield of faith, with which you can extinguish all the flaming arrows of the evil one. And take the helmet of salvation and the sword of the Spirit, which is the word of God. Pray in the Spirit at all times, with every kind of prayer and petition. To this end, stay alert with all perseverance in your prayers for all the saints.

Ephesians 6:13-18

The Roman soldier wore sandals that usually had spikes on the soles and were laced with leather high up the leg to be able to stand firmly and be more sure-footed. Men and women preparing to do their military jobs have different types of boots—some with cleats to grab terrain, some with steel toes to protect from heavy equipment, and all with ankle support to help them stand firm. The boots in the armor of God are made of peace. Wait. What? How can boots of peace help me to stand firm against the enemy? Charles Swindoll describes it well:

The boots of peace (6:15). I'm sure Paul had spent many long hours looking at his jailer's boots, called *caligae*. . . Our "footing" against Satan is our peace with God. Christ has secured this peace for us (Eph. 2)—peace not only with God but also with one another and within ourselves. As a result of this peace, our Lord will never condemn us (Rom. 8:1). Satan may pressure us all he wants, trying to convince us that God will reject and judge us when we falter. But if we know that our peace with God is secure, then we won't slip and fall. We'll stand stable and firm against the devil's taunts. Moreover, we'll gain ground against his opposition so that we can spread the good news of peace with God through Christ to the troubled world around us. (84)

Boots of peace protect us and enable us to stand against Satan by appropriating what Jesus bought for us by His sacrifice on the cross to satisfy the wrath of God against our sin. We can stand firm on the truth that the penalty for our sin, the death sentence, has already been placed on Jesus. Therefore, the enemy—Satan—can no longer accuse us of sin. The accusation is null and void, of no consequence, because the soap of Jesus's love—His own blood—washed away anything that could be used to condemn us. We can stand strongly because Jesus is our peace.

When Satan tries to make you feel condemnation, strap on your boots of peace! Then walk in those boots to share His peace with others!

Father, help us to put on Your armor to face each day. Help us to lace up those shoes of peace tightly and walk in confidence that we are at peace with You through Christ and can experience personal peace and peace with others as well.

Sing along with Don Moen's "No Condemnation". Yes, the song is repeated numerous times, but if you keep singing it, you will internalize and possibly memorize Romans 8:1-2
https://www.youtube.com/watch?v=GOqEf1Xv3jw

Romans 8:1-2 (NASB 1995) *Therefore there is now no condemnation for those who are in Christ Jesus. For the law of the Spirit of life in Christ Jesus has set you free from the law of sin and of death.*

PEACE PROGRESSES FROM GOD'S LOVE

Peace^{G1515} to the brothers and love^{G26} with faith from God the Father and the Lord Jesus Christ. Grace to all who love our Lord Jesus Christ with an undying love.

Ephesians 6:23-24

As Paul beautifully began his letter, so he eloquently closes it. He extends a blessing of peace, love, and faith from God the Father and the Lord Jesus (6:23). It's almost as though Paul were summing up the main themes of the entire letter to the Ephesians. Since Christ has established peace with God and between believers (2:14–15), those called by His name are to live out that peace, "being diligent to preserve the unity of the Spirit in the bond of peace" (4:3). This peaceful way of life was first on Paul's mind, and close behind it was love—the basis for achieving peace. (85)

Ephesians finishes with a truly apostolic benediction, but one different in form from others in Paul's writings. Couched in the third person, not in the second, it has two parts instead of one. "Grace," which usually comes first, stands last. The three blessings that figure most prominently throughout Ephesians—peace, love, and faith—occupy the first half of the benediction. This is more than a farewell greeting; it is a prayer for reconciliation. Paul longs to see the whole brotherhood of believers in Ephesus and its environs— Jews and Gentiles alike—at "peace" with each other in the one body of Christ (3:15, 19; 4:3). This will only be brought about through mutual "love" (1:15; 3:17-18; 4:2, 16) combined with "faith," from which it is derived (1:15; 3:17; Gal 5:6). The ultimate source of these three essential features of Christian community life is God himself. The name of Christ the Son is associated with that of God the Father in perfect equality. (86)

The foundation for peace and unity in the local church as well as the church worldwide is the love that fills us and flows through us when we place our faith in Christ. If we are living examples of agápē, we will be living at peace with our brothers and sisters in Christ.

G26 agápē – Spoken more especially of good will toward others, the love of our neighbor, brotherly affection, which the Lord Jesus commands and inspires (John 15:13; 17:26; Rom. 13:10; 1 Cor. 13:1; Heb. 6:10; 1 John 4:7). In 2 Cor. 13:11, "the God of love" means the author and source of love, who Himself is love. In Rom. 15:30, "the love of the Spirit" means that love which the Spirit inspires. (87)

When we truly love others, we will consistently treat them as we would like to be treated (Luke 6:31). Wouldn't that behavior help us to live in peace? Throughout Ephesians and in many of his other letters, Paul urges believers to live in unity, harmony, peace with each other. That is only possible as the Holy Spirit instills Christ-like love in us, and we allow it to flow through us. All the Fruit of the Spirit must be cultivated and nurtured. In other words, we must learn what the Bible says about each characteristic, then practice it until we internalize it. We are to be in the process of becoming more and more like Jesus. The Fruit of Spirit should be evident in our daily lives and should become our natural response—like breathing—rather than something we must think about and struggle to do.

Is it your natural response to make every effort to keep the peace with other believers? Do you consistently respond in love? We all need to evaluate how we are doing by checking our attitudes and actions against the Fruit of the Spirit in Galatians 5:22-23. When we fall short by reacting rather than responding, we need to ask the Lord to forgive us and strengthen us in the areas in which we struggle.

Father, none of us will reach perfection this side of Heaven. However, You are continuing to perfect and complete the work You began in each of us (Philippians 1:6). Help us to live in unity, harmony, peace with other believers, especially those in the local body of Christ in which we serve.

221

Worship with Kristyn Getty, Margaret Becker, and Jo-anne Hogg singing "May the Peace of God": https://www.youtube.com/watch?v=QQlFHIRFGGU&list=RD-QQlFHIRFGGU&start_radio=1

PREVAILING PEACE

Be anxious for nothing, but in everything, by prayer and petition, with thanksgiving, present your requests to God. And the peace^{G1515} of God, which surpasses all understanding, will guard your hearts and your minds in Christ Jesus.

Philippians 4:6-7

On the day I called, You answered me; You emboldened me and strengthened my soul.

Psalm 138:3

When sores began cropping up on my feet, I did not understand the depth of the problem. They began creeping up my legs despite the doctors' best efforts to cure them and my family's efforts with home remedies. I had only short periods of relief before they returned with a vengeance. I realized the seriousness of the problem when the doctors scraped the wounds to do a culture and nothing definitive came back. They did not have a name for what was causing these necrotic ulcers and were unable to come up with an effective treatment plan. I cried out to the Lord for healing, but physical healing did not occur in the way I had hoped. My feet looked like they were rotting or melting, and in essence, they were! One doctor said that sepsis and even dying were possibilities that could occur at any time. In fact, he described my legs with the terrifying words, "Two ticking time-bombs!" The Lord gave me the strength and peace I needed to make the decision to have both legs amputated. On one hand, it was a heart-wrenching decision; but on the other hand, it was a "no-brainer." It was only in Jesus Christ that I could make this choice, and His peace prevailed even during the difficult time of recovery. Because I had peace with God, I was given the peace of God.

Not every time we cry out to the Lord is this drastic, but we can be assured that the Lord hears our cry. We can be certain that the Lord is with us, and as long as He is with us, we can have the peace to face any challenge. He has the power to bring us out of or through our situation when we rest in Him as our Prince of Peace. What are you crying out to the Lord about today? Thank Him in advance for the answer and the peace He will provide.

Father, we are able to obediently thank You for all things because we know You will provide peace in our lives despite our circumstances.

Worship along with Mercy Me singing "Bring the Rain": https://www.youtube.com/watch?v=e8HgAVenbUU and Mercy Me singing "Even If": https://www.youtube.com/watch?v=B6fA35Ved-Y

Or memorize a paraphrase of this Scripture by listening to this lullaby: https://www.youtube.com/watch?v=Q4Af1zhUPxs

FOCUS ON PRECIOUS PERCEPTIONS

Finally, brothers, whatever is true, whatever is honorable, whatever is right, whatever is pure, whatever is lovely, whatever is admirable—if anything is excellent or praiseworthy—think on these things. Whatever you have learned or received or heard from me, or seen in me, put it into practice. And the God of peace[G1515] will be with you.

Philippians 4:8-9

In Philippians 4:6-7, Paul exhorts the reader that instead of being anxious or fretting, the believer needs to turn their concerns over to the Lord in prayer with thanksgiving in order to have that peace of mind that most people will never understand. The only way to experience this type of peace is to trust in Christ as Savior and rest in the truth that God is in control. Christ is our peace. Paul continues this theme of how to replace anxiety and worry with peace in verses 8 and 9. We must change our thinking. Often our thought patterns dwell on the bad news of the day, the difficulties we have encountered, the day-to-day struggles we all face. However, we can change our mindset by placing those thoughts at the foot of the cross and leaving them there. But the next step is to replace the "stinking thinking" with "precious perceptions." We are to think on things that are:

- True – God's Word

- Honorable – Good deeds, kindness, noble deeds
- Right – Justice, fairness
- Pure – Untarnished, undefiled, clean
- Lovely – Beautiful, caring, gracious
- Admirable – Authenticity, tenacity, consistency
- Excellent – Skilled, expert, achieving high standards
- Praiseworthy – Good, strong work ethic, accountability

Then, Paul encourages them to remember what he has taught them and what they have seen him do and emulate him, follow his example. The way he lived his life out before them was an example of following and obeying Jesus. We may not have Paul with us in person, but we have his letters. However, we have Christian examples that we would do good to imitate. Susan and I have often complained that we got a late start in ministry together since she was 48 and I was 58 when we first began working together; but God has placed examples in our lives to show us that He is not through with us. We have a "coach"—spiritual mentor—who is 94 years young! We have a dear sister in the Lord who is the picture of hospitality and generosity who is in her eighties! We need to focus on the positive and live for Christ, really LIVE until the day He calls us home!

How is your thought life? Do you dwell on dread, or do you focus on finishing well? Do you fill your mind with all the bad news, or do you purposefully ponder truth, beauty, love, kindness, etc.? We need to make a practice of pondering the positive! We will be much more inclined to relax in the peace God provides when we change our thinking to be in line with His.

Father, help us daily to take Your prescription for peace by placing our cares on You and focusing our mind on the best things rather than the worst.

Worship along with the Gaither Vocal Band singing "Everything Good": https://www.youtube.com/watch?v=jJu7rOv-c8M

GRACE AND PEACE AS A GREETING

Paul, an apostle of Christ Jesus by the will of God, and Timothy our brother, To the saints and faithful brothers in Christ at Colossae: Grace and peace[G1515] *to you from God our Father.*

Colossians 1:1-2

As with the letter to the Ephesians, Paul was writing to believers, those who had trusted Jesus, at Colossae and then at Laodicea, as many of his letters were read in one place then shared with another church. Paul indicated that Timothy was with him and sent greetings as well. Paul was not a loner. He often worked as a team with another minister. In fact, Timothy was one of Paul's spiritual children, a man he had discipled and helped to grow in his faith to the point that he ultimately sent Timothy out to pastor a church. Paul extended his usual greeting to the recipients of the letter by pronouncing grace and peace to them from the Lord.

G5485 Charis – . . .graciousness of manner or act: lit. fig., or spiritual; especially the divine influence upon the heart, and its reflection in the life . . (88)

G1515 eirénē, i-ray'-nay; probably from a primary verb eírō (to join); peace (literally or figuratively); by implication, prosperity:—one, peace,
quietness, rest, + set at one again. (89)

G5485 cháris – (III) (B) Of the grace, favor and
goodwill of God and Christ as exercised toward
men: where cháris is joined with eiréné (1515),
peace, éleos (1656), mercy, and the like in salu-
tations, including the idea of every kind of favor,
blessing, good, as proceeding from God the Father and the Lord Jesus Christ (Rom. 1:7; 1 Cor
1:3; 2 Cor 1:2; Gal. 1:3). Also, in the introduction
to most of the epistles (Eph 1:2; Phil. 1:2; Col.
1:2; 1 Thess. 1:1; 2 Thess. 1:2; 1 Tim. 1:2, Titus
1:4, Phile. 1:3; 1 Pet. 1:2, 2 Pet. 1:2; 2 John 1:3;
Rev. 1:4). (90)

Grace as defined above was asking the Lord to effect
transformation in their lives and bestow blessings on
them. With the word peace, Paul was indicating his desire that the Lord set their lives in order, make them
whole, and give them rest. He was believing the Lord
would extend every kind of blessing to them. Perhaps we
need to revive this greeting in our own letters, emails, or
when we meet up with our Christian friends.

In your opinion, could we revive the greeting of "Grace
and peace to you from God the Father?" Why or why
not? Could we use this greeting with non-believers or
with Christians only?

Father, let us pray for Your grace and peace in other believers' lives. Let it not just be a way to begin a letter or greet a friend but our true prayer for them.

Pronouncing a blessing was not new to the Apostle Paul. We find a benediction that has been set to music many times in Numbers 6:24-26. Listen to one of our favorite settings. By the way, if you memorize this song, you have memorized Scripture!
https://www.youtube.com/watch?v=Nxn6tmVSljU
"The Lord Bless You and Keep You" by the Altar of Praise Chorale

THE SON BLED PEACE INTO THE WORLD

He is the exact image of the invisible God, the firstborn of creation, the eternal. It was by Him that everything was created: the heavens, the earth, all things within and upon them, all things seen and unseen, thrones and dominions, spiritual powers and authorities. Every detail was crafted through His design, by His own hands, and for His purposes. He has always been! It is His hand that holds everything together. He is the head of this body, the church. He is the beginning, the first of those to be reborn from the dead, so that in every aspect, at every view, in everything—He is first. God was pleased that all His fullness should forever dwell in the Son who, as predetermined by God, bled peace[G1517] into the world by His death on the cross as God's means of reconciling to Himself the whole creation—all things in heaven and all things on earth.

Colossians 1:15-20 (VOICE)

1:15–20 One component in the heresy threatening the Colossian church was the denial of the deity of Christ. Paul combats that damning element of heresy with an emphatic defense of Christ's deity. (91)

Jesus is the exact image of God meaning the incarnate Jesus was God in a form man could see. However, Jesus has also existed eternally and not only was present at creation but was, indeed, the one who created everything, spoke the world into being, breathed life into Adam, and is still the glue that holds everything together. If one planet strayed a tiny amount out of its orbit, the entire solar system might end up colliding. Jesus not only orders our lives but is the one who makes sure that everything in the universe stays on course! He is the firstborn from the dead meaning that he is the first person resurrected to never die again, and we will follow Him into that life if we have trusted in Him on this earth. In everything, Jesus is first, before, or in some translations "preeminent". Jesus is before all things in the sense that he was present at creation. He is first in the sense that he is supreme, above all things.

Colossians 1:15–23 contains the apostle Paul's counterargument against false teachings about the nature and divinity of Jesus Christ. This important section of Scripture is given titles such as "The Preeminence of Christ" (ESV) or "The Supremacy of the Son of God" (NIV). False teachers were claiming that Jesus may have been prominent but not the foremost, highest-ranking being in all creation. As part of his case, Paul stated, "He [Jesus] is before all things" (Colossians 1:17, ESV), meaning Jesus Christ existed before anything else was created. Since only God can exist before all of creation, Paul affirmed that Jesus Christ is God. (92)

All of God's "fullness" was in Jesus meaning that he was equal in power with God the Father. Jesus was fully God and fully human at the same time, a concept difficult for our finite minds to grasp. He needed to be human in order to meet the qualifications of being the perfect, sinless, spotless Lamb of God. God provided His own sacrifice to make peace with us. Jesus's purpose in becoming a man was to reconcile people to God. To do that, he had to satisfy the righteous wrath of God by being our substitute on the cross. We deserved the death penalty for our sin, our disobedience to God. Truly, we were filthy, covered in our sin and incapable of making ourselves right with God. Jesus "bled peace into the world" by his sacrifice on the cross. His blood is the only cleansing agent capable of removing the stain of sin from our lives. Jesus, in his love for us, chose to lay down his life in order to wash away everything that would separate us from God forever. The only way to have peace with God is to trust in, rely on, Jesus's finished work on the cross, surrendering our lives to His control. Just as Jesus was raised from the dead to have a new body that could never die, so will we be given a new body like His when we are resurrected from the dead to live in peace with God forever.

Do you have peace with God? That is the beginning point in order to have any other kind of peace. If you are not absolutely sure that your sins are forgiven and Jesus is preparing a place for you (John 14:1-3), please turn to the "Jewels of Salvation" section in this book and/or contact a Bible teaching pastor, Sunday school teacher, or Christian friend to discuss in full how you can have peace with God. If you already have peace with God, you now have the responsibility and privilege of sharing that Good News with others! Remember: Jesus came to give us abundant life, a life full of peace, love, and joy!

John 10:10 (AMP) *The thief comes only in order to steal and kill and destroy. I came that they may have and enjoy life, and have it in abundance [to the full, till it overflows].*

Father, we thank you that our lives are made full and joyful because we have trusted in Christ's completed work on the cross and believed in His resurrection from the dead. Thank You that this abundant life cannot be stolen by Satan because You hold us securely in Your hand. (John 10:27-30).

Worship along with Casting Crowns singing "Who Am I?": https://www.youtube.com/watch?v=mBcqria2w-mg&list=RDmBcqria2wmg&start_radio=1

LET GOD'S PEACE REIGN AND BE THANKFUL!

Let the peace[G1515] of Christ rule in your hearts, for to this you were called as members of one body. And be thankful. Let the word of Christ richly dwell within you as you teach and admonish one another with all wisdom, and as you sing psalms, hymns, and spiritual songs with gratitude in your hearts to God. And whatever you do, in word or deed, do it all in the name of the Lord Jesus, giving thanks to God the Father through Him.

Colossians 3:15-17

God is sovereign, is completely in charge, and when we surrender our all to Him, we will have the peace and confidence to live in harmonious community with our brothers and sisters in Christ. There will be peace in the "familyship" as we each have the peace of submission and obedience to the Lord ruling in our individual hearts and lives. The word of God is our instruction manual, our life-coach, the source of continuity in living for Jesus. As we fully immerse ourselves, soaking in the Scripture, we will not only have peace ourselves but will be able to encourage others to live and dwell in peace by abiding in the word. As the word begins to seep into and overflow our being, the Lord will infuse us with the power to accomplish all He has called us to do in the grace of and to the glory of God. When we are steeped in the peace of God, all that we desire is to be an overflowing reservoir of gratitude and thanksgiving.

When the teabag is sitting in the hot water, it is "steeping." The longer is steeps, the stronger the flavor of the tea. We need to be steeped in God's word in order to maintain peace in our own lives and with others. In order to be enabled to share God's peace with others, we need to "sit in" the water of His Word, until we are saturated with it. Are you steeping in the Bible each day, not just reading a passage to check off your daily Bible reading quota, but truly soaking it in until you are "flavored" with His peace?

Father, may our hearts burst out in songs of praise and thanksgiving as we realize the peace that passes all understanding has been bountifully accredited to our accounts because Jesus paid the price of our sin on the cross and was raised from the dead. Thank You, Lord, that Your peace permeates our lives in such a way that we need not live in fear, and we can share peace with others.

Worship along with the Classic Hymns Mass Choir singing Leonard Smith's song "Our God Reigns":
https://www.youtube.com/watch?v=_y7z3dRrtiU

Let the peace^{G1515} of Christ rule in your hearts, for to this you were called as members of one body. And be thankful. Let the word of Christ richly dwell within you as you teach and admonish one another with all wisdom, and as you sing psalms, hymns, and spiritual songs with gratitude in your hearts to God. And whatever you do, in word or deed, do it all in the name of the Lord Jesus, giving thanks to God the Father through Him.

Colossians 3:15-17

MAY YOUR PEACE REIGN

May your peace, Lord, reign in us.
Let your word inhabit our minds.
Allow us to teach with wisdom,
so that others in Your word will find
the peace that they have craved, Lord.
Then with a full heart they may sing.
May gratitude flow from our hearts, Lord,
as an offering of worship we bring.

LIVE IN PEACE WITH LEADERS

But we ask you, brothers, to acknowledge those who work diligently among you, who preside over you in the Lord and give you instruction. In love, hold them in highest[G4057] regard because of their work. Live in peace[G1514] with one another.

1 Thessalonians 5:12-13

G4057 perissōs, per-is-soce'; adverb from G4053; superabundantly:—exceedingly, out of measure, the more. (93)

5:12–13 Paul ends the letter by speaking more generally to the whole church. The first topic he addresses is their attitude toward leaders. The Thessalonians are to acknowledge, esteem highly, and be at peace with those who lead. In essence they are to be loyal to them. The leadership is defined not by office here but by activity. The leaders work among them and over them, and they admonish them. Paul assumes a leadership structure, but this leadership is among the people, walking alongside them in the faith. (94)

5:12, 13 In spite of their limitations, God's spiritual leaders should be respected and obeyed—unless it is obvious that they are out of God's will. As the spiritual leaders of the church meet together, plan, pray, and seek and follow God's will, we can be sure that God will rule and over-rule in the decisions they make. The result of the church family following the spiritual leaders will be peace and harmony in the church. (95)

With all the headlines today about pastors and other church leaders who are blatantly not in line with God's will, it may be difficult to hold leadership in high regard, showing respect and esteem. However, we cannot judge one person by another person's failures. We must show respect and work well with our church leadership unless and until a man or woman proves to be out of God's will. Our pastors and teachers carry a high responsibility:

James 3:1 (AMP) *Not many [of you] should become teachers [serving in an official teaching capacity], my brothers and sisters, for you know that we [who are teachers] will be judged by a higher standard [because we have assumed greater accountability and more condemnation if we teach incorrectly].*

Since the leaders in our churches carry such a responsibility, we should pray diligently for them! We should not only treat them with respect but make every effort to encourage them. If we feel our pastor or other leader is in error, we need to practice what is laid out in Matthew 18:15-17, namely 1) go to the person in question and lovingly confront them to give them an opportunity to correct it, 2) if one-on-one does not work, take ONE or TWO other believers with you as witnesses to the conversation, 3) if a person still does not see the error of their ways, take it before the church. By all means, do not gossip about any suspicion you may have!

Do you treat your leaders in the church with respect? If you do not think they have earned respect or have lost it, do you go to them individually and give them a chance to respond? Do you pray for your pastors and leaders regularly and diligently? Do you give them an encouraging word in person, by text, by email, or in a greeting card? Are you at peace with your spiritual leaders?

Father, thank You for our pastors and their support staff. Thank you for the teachers of our small groups. Help us to remember to lift them up in prayer and to encourage them often. Help us to be more consistent in showing them we care about them and appreciate how much they show us Your love.

GOD OF PEACE HIMSELF SANCTIFIES US

Now may the God of peace^{G1515} Himself sanctify^{G37} you completely, and may your entire spirit, soul, and body be kept blameless at the coming of our Lord Jesus Christ. The One who calls you is faithful, and He will do it.

1 Thessalonians 5:23-24

G37 37. hagiázō; fut. hagiásō, from hágios (40), holy. To make holy, sanctify.

(I) To make clean, render pure.

(A) Particularly in Heb. 9:13.

(B) Metaphorically, to render clean in a moral sense, to purify, sanctify (Rom. 15:16, "being sanctified by the Holy Ghost," meaning by the sanctifying influences of the Holy Spirit on the heart. See 1 Cor. 6:11; Eph. 5:26; 1 Thess. 5:23; 1 Tim. 4:5; Heb. 2:11; 10:10, 14, 29; 13:12; Rev. 22:11). (96)

Paul points out that sanctification is ultimately God's work in us, not our work for him. Yes, we are active in yielding to the power of the Spirit and depending on His gracious and powerful provision, but it is ultimately God who is working in us "both to will and to work for His good pleasure" (Phil. 2:12–13) (97)

In concluding his letter to the church at Thessalonica, Paul pronounced a blessing on them. He prayed the

"God of Peace" Himself would sanctify them—cleanse them and set them apart for His service. Peace indicates far more than calmness or absence of trouble. The word used encompasses the Old Testament idea of shalom—nothing missing, nothing broken, completely whole. God takes our brokenness and makes us whole. He washes away our sinfulness and purifies us by placing His Holy Spirit within us to guide us. It is God Himself who restores our peace and makes us holy. God Himself has called us to trust in Jesus:

John 6:44 (NLT) *For no one can come to me unless the Father who sent me draws them to me, and at the last day I will raise them up.*

God is also the One who sanctifies us, purifies us, prepares us to live with Him forever. God is faithful to do what He promises. He plans to make us more like Jesus which is sanctification.

Romans 8:28-30 *And we know that God works all things together for the good of those who love Him, who are called according to His purpose. For those God foreknew, He also predestined to be conformed to the image of His Son, so that He would be the firstborn among many brothers. And those He predestined, He also called; those He called, He also justified; those He justified, He also glorified.*

God has a plan for us, and it is He who enables us to fulfill His plan. He revealed to Jeremiah that He had chosen and set him apart to be His prophet before he was even born!

Jeremiah 1:4-5 (NLT) *The Lord gave me this message: "I knew you before I formed you in your mother's womb. Before you were born I set you apart and appointed you as my prophet to the nations."*

If you know Jesus as your Lord, you have a God given purpose as well. His Holy Spirit indwells you in order to guide you and sanctify you for service. Ask the Lord to show you how best to fulfill His purposes in your life. Then act in obedience to what the Holy Spirit reveals through Scripture and prayer. God will be faithful to make sure you finish well:

Philippians 1:6 (NLT) *And I am certain that God, who began the good work within you, will continue his work until it is finally finished on the day when Christ Jesus returns.*

Father, thank You that since we cannot possibly make ourselves holy, You Yourself sanctify us and keep us at peace with You. You will empower us to fulfill Your purpose in us. We simply need to lean into You, listen to the Holy Spirit's promptings, and move in obedience to Your will and ways.

Worship along with Steve Green singing "He Who Began a Good Work in You": https://www.youtube.com/watch?v=eNjZlHARnEk

Be encouraged by Gloria Trotter singing "He'll Do It Again": https://www.youtube.com/watch?v=UN9Jsk-CHlXg&list=RDUN9JskCHlXg&start_radio=1

PEACE ALWAYS IN ALL WAYS

Now may the Lord of peace^{G1515} Himself grant you His peace^{G1515} (the peace^{G1515} of His kingdom) at all times and in all ways [under all circumstances and conditions, whatever comes]. The Lord [be] with you all.

2 Thessalonians 3:16 (AMPC)

3:16 You know you're where God wants you to be when you are objectively in his Word and he subjectively confirms it with his peace. Peace is harmony on the inside always in every way—that is, regardless of your circumstances. (98)

3:16 The peace of God is a gift; it is not something we can manipulate because it is the fruit of oneness with Him. When our relationship with Him is strong and adversity strikes, we do not have to fall apart or give in to anxiety. We can choose to live in steadfast confidence of His love, wisdom, power, and provision. This is the basis of His unshakable peace—not that we are capable of controlling circumstances, but that His help is ever-present and perfect to deliver us in every challenge we face. (99)

A s Charles Stanley wrote above, peace "is the fruit of oneness with Him." Peace is indeed the power of God's presence within us in the person of the Holy Spirit. The ability to remain calm when all about us is in chaos is, indeed, a powerful position. What is amazing is that God's peace is His gift to us! We do not strive to achieve the peace of God because even if we worked really hard at it, His peace would be impossible to obtain on our own. We rest on His promises rather than wrestle with what ifs. Once we are at peace with God by trusting in Christ's death in our place on the cross, we have access to the peace of God. How do we engage God's peace when faced with difficulties and even overwhelming circumstances? We talk to the Giver of Peace, God Himself. The word for talking with God is prayer. In Philippians we learned the key to peace:

Philippians 4:6-7 (NLT) *Don't worry about anything; instead, pray about everything. Tell God what you need, and thank him for all he has done. Then you will experience God's peace, which exceeds anything we can understand. His peace will guard your hearts and minds as you live in Christ Jesus.*

Do you struggle to maintain composure when everything seems to be falling apart? We do, but when we remember to "take it to the Lord in prayer" as the old hymn says, our peace is restored. Whatever is disturbing your tranquility needs to transferred to the Lord. Let Him handle all your problems.

1 Peter 5:7 (VOICE) *Since God cares for you, let Him carry all your burdens and worries.*

Father, it has been a stressful week, and at times we were slow in turning that stress over to You. Please forgive us when we fail to remember that we can turn every care over to You. Right now, we choose to rest in the assurance that You are taking care of every burden, every concern, every problem that we have. We are Your daughters, and we know that You as our Father want us to bring all these things to You and let You handle them.

Worship along with Alan Jackson singing "What a Friend We Have in Jesus" which is a reminder to "Take it to the Lord in Prayer": https://www.youtube.com/watch?v=znWu2HCJ92c

GRACE, MERCY, AND PEACE

To Timothy, my true child in the faith: Grace, mercy, and peace[G1515] from God the Father and Christ Jesus our Lord.

1 Timothy 1:2

Paul, an apostle of Christ Jesus by the will of God, according to the promise of life in Christ Jesus, To Timothy, my beloved child: Grace, mercy, and peace[G1515] from God the Father and Christ Jesus our Lord.

2 Timothy 1:1-2

First and Second Timothy are labeled "Pastoral Epistles." Many of Paul's letters were to churches, entire congregations; but in these letters, he is writing to Timothy, his son in the faith. Timothy had been sent out by Paul as a young pastor to the church at Ephesus. He was strong in the Lord because Paul had discipled him and may have even led him to the Lord. Paul continued to mentor Timothy by sending him letters as he did with Titus. In both letters, Paul greeted Timothy with "Grace, mercy, and peace from God the Father and Christ Jesus our Lord."

> 1 Timothy 1:2 Grace, mercy and peace. "Grace" and "peace" are part of Paul's greetings in all his letters; here and in 2 Timothy 1:2 he adds "mercy" (cf. 2 John 3; Jude 2). Certain circumstances may call for an explicit sense that God is present and bestowing his favor. (100)

Paul had more faith in Timothy at times than Timothy had in himself. Paul saw Timothy's potential. Although Timothy was a young man, God had given him specific spiritual gifts needed in a pastor. In 1 Timothy, Paul gave him instruction in how to run a church, and in 2 Timothy, he instructs his young mentee in how to be an effective pastor. Paul had to encourage young Timothy to be assertive in his authority as a pastor saying:

1 Timothy 4:12 *Don't let anyone belittle you because you are young. Instead, show the faithful, young and old, an example of how to live: set the standard for how to talk, act, love, and be faithful and pure.*

Timothy was to lead by his own example. He was to model becoming more and more like Jesus for the believers at Ephesus. He would definitely need God's grace, mercy, and peace in order to relentlessly pursue growing in Christlikeness in a city where most citizens engaged in the worship of Artemis, the patroness of sexual instinct. For the Apostle Paul, "grace, mercy, and peace" were not just a pleasant way to greet Timothy in the letters but were his constant, continual prayer on Timothy's behalf.

Do you have a younger believer that you mentor (disciple)? If so, do you pray for God to give them increasing measures of grace, mercy, and peace? Do you have someone who has been that kind of mentor for you? Be sure to thank God for them!

Father, thank You for the many people in our lives who have encouraged us, taught us, mentored us, and prayed for us. Help us to be faithful prayer warriors for those who look to us as teachers. Grant us all Your grace, mercy, and peace for each day.

HUNT DOWN HARMONY

Shun youthful lusts and flee from them, and aim at and pursue righteousness (all that is virtuous and good, right living, conformity to the will of God in thought, word, and deed); [and aim at and pursue] faith, love, [and] peace[G1515] *(harmony and concord with others) in fellowship with all [Christians], who call upon the Lord out of a pure heart.*

2 Timothy 2:22 (AMPC)

False teachers had stirred up strife, and disagreements were rampant in Ephesus where Timothy pastored. Paul urged Timothy to pursue peace. He was to seek harmony and unity, agreement between parties when possible. Paul gave this same instruction to the church at Rome: Romans 12:18 (ESV), "If possible, so far as it depends on you, live peaceably with all." Can we live in harmony, in unity, with those whose opinions differ greatly from our own? Not always, but most of the time, especially if both parties are believers. If two people are willing to hear each other out, there can always be harmony but not necessarily agreement. Harmony can be "agreeing to disagree" and continuing to fellowship because the disagreement is something peripheral and not essential to the truth of the Gospel message of salvation through Christ alone. Harmony in a choir involves people singing different notes that complement one another, are concordant together. As a church, we are not all singing melody, we are not in unison (on the same note); but we must be in unity, harmony with one another. If the tone becomes discordant in the church as well as music, it will not sound pleasant until it is resolved. Resolution is not always singing the exact same note but is making sure the two notes do not clash. If you are in a state of discord, disharmony, with another believer, work to resolve the problem and restore the relationship to peace.

Pursue—hunt down—harmony. Pray the Lord will help you to live at peace with everyone as far as it depends on you. You cannot control another person's response, but you are responsible for and can control your own.

Father, grant us the self-control necessary to pursue peace with others!

GRACE AND PEACE
TO PHILEMON

Paul, a prisoner of Christ Jesus, and Timothy our brother, To Philemon our beloved fellow worker, to Apphia our sister, to Archippus our fellow soldier, and to the church that meets at your house: Grace and peace^{G1515} to you from God our Father and the Lord Jesus Christ.

Philemon 1:1-3

First let's examine the people mentioned in the salutation of this letter. Of course, we know who the Apostle Paul is, and that Timothy was his "son in the faith." At this time, Timothy was in Rome to encourage Paul who was imprisoned there. The letter is addressed primarily to Philemon who had a church meeting in his home. Philemon owned a slave named Onesimus who had run away, but Paul had led Onesimus to the Lord and urged him to return to his master, Philemon. Paul had Onesimus deliver this letter in person. Apphia was Philemon's wife, and Archippus was either his son or an elder in the church that met in his home. If he were an elder, Paul may have addressed the letter to him as well as Philemon; so that Philemon would be held accountable for considering Paul's advice. The letter was also to be read to the entire congregation that met in Philemon's home.

Before Paul delves into the meat of his letter, he pronounces his usual blessing over Philemon, his household, and the church that met there: "Grace and Peace from God our Father and the Lord Jesus Christ." Paul's linking of the Lord Jesus Christ with God our Father indicated that Jesus was equal to God. We noticed that instead of "God the Father," in the letter to Philemon, Paul wrote "God our Father." Perhaps the use of "our" instead of "the" is to call attention to the fact that Philemon and Onesimus shared the same relationship to God since Onesimus had come to Jesus under Paul's ministry. Paul's letter to Philemon was personal, practical, and pertinent to the situation between Philemon and the runaway slave named Onesimus which means "useful." Onesimus had actually become "useless" since he had not only run away from service to Philemon but had stolen from him! Paul was asking Philemon to accept Onesimus back as a "brother."

> Clearly, Paul's letter to Philemon has great practical value for us today. It illustrates for us the reality and importance of second chances, the equality that believers have in Christ, and the power of the gospel to transcend cultural and social boundaries. In short, Paul's postcard to Philemon reminds us about the profoundly Christ-centered concepts of freedom, forgiveness, mercy, and grace … especially grace. (101)

We can be confident that Philemon did exactly as Paul requested because history shows that Onesimus eventually became the bishop of Ephesus! God took him from being a useless runaway slave to being a man used for God's glory as a leader in the early church. It seems that ultimately Onesimus lived up to his name!

> Who was the bishop of this prominent church in the early second century? A man named Onesimus. In a letter sent to the church in Ephesus to encourage them in their faithfulness to Christ, Ignatius described their bishop, Onesimus, as "a man of inexpressible love," adding, "Blessed is the one who has graciously granted you, who are worthy, to obtain such a bishop. (102)

Grace, mercy, and peace. Do we remember to pray these three things for our fellow servants of Jesus? Do we encourage one another to forgive a brother or sister in Christ like Paul did Philemon? Paul even offered to make restitution on behalf of Onesimus if Philemon asked him to! May we learn the lessons of acceptance and forgiveness even while holding someone accountable. All of these things are easy to say or write but challenging to do. We can only put the lessons of this letter into practice by the power of the Holy Spirit within us.

Father, help us to practice and apply the lessons we have learned in preparing this book about peace.

Worship with the Bill Gaither Trio featuring Bill and Gloria Gaither and Gary McSpadden singing "I am Loved": https://www.youtube.com/watch?v=K3vGN6BP4eI

Susan Slade and Susie Hale

DISCIPLINE YIELDS THE PEACEFUL FRUIT OF RIGHTEOUSNESS

. . . we had physical fathers who disciplined us, and we respected them; how much more should we submit to our spiritual Father and live! For they disciplined us only for a short time and only as best they could; but he disciplines us in a way that provides genuine benefit to us and enables us to share in his holiness. Now, all discipline, while it is happening, does indeed seem painful, not enjoyable; but for those who have been trained by it, it later produces its peaceful[G1516] *fruit, which is righteousness.*

Hebrews 12:9-11 (CJB)

When God disciplines us, it is proof positive that He is our Father who loves us. Good earthly fathers train their children with positive affirmations and negative consequences. Negative consequences do not feel good when we are undergoing them. However, they can have a positive effect on our character. The same is true with our Heavenly Father's discipline. Sometimes He allows a difficulty in our lives to get our focus back on Him. He may use trials to strengthen us and help us to learn to rely more on Him.

Whatever the experience, we can be sure that His hand of discipline is controlled by His loving heart. The Father does not want us to be pampered babies; He wants us to become mature adult sons and daughters who can be trusted with the responsibilities of life. (103)

God's discipline produces in us a peaceful harvest of righteous living. What does this mean? When we live in obedience to Christ's commands, respond to the Father's discipline by making necessary course corrections, and grow more and more like the image of God's son, we will have true peace. There is no greater peace than being confident we are in the center of God's will. We are not righteous through our own efforts but because Jesus imparts His righteousness to us. However, we should be constantly, consistently cultivating the Fruit of the Spirit, the evidence of responding to the Father's loving discipline in our lives. Only human beings are created in God's image. In discussing God's command to Adam not to eat of the Tree of the Knowledge of Good and Evil, Steve Green writes:

Only man, of all creation, was given this instruction; human beings alone were given moral choice. (104)

Because God gave us the ability to choose, He lovingly disciplines and guides us toward righteousness. We can go kicking and screaming if we choose, or we can submit to God's will and proceed peacefully. The choice is ours.

Father, help us to respond quickly to the Holy Spirit's promptings, to conviction when we have strayed from

Your path. The Enemy seeks to condemn us; but in Your mercy and grace, You lift us up and train us in righteousness. Help us to be diligent in following Jesus and living out Your commands daily.

PURSUE PEACE

Make every effort to live in peace^{G1515} with everyone and to be holy; without holiness no one will see the Lord.

Hebrews 12:14

12:14 Make every effort. The author calls for renewed focus (as in 2:1; 4:11; 6:1; 10:24–25) on "peace" and "holiness." The context of vv. 10b–13 shows that God produces these in us through Christ (see 2:11; 10:10, 14; 13:12); he enables us to choose wise pathways (3:14; 7:25; 8:10; 9:13–15; 13:20–21). Only those who are holy in this way "will see the Lord" (i.e., commune with him in the new heaven and new earth, Ps 17:15; Matt 5:8; Rev 22:4). (105)

We have seen previously that we are to work at living peacefully with everyone as far as it depends on us:

Romans 12:18 (CJB) *If possible, and to the extent that it depends on you, live in peace with all people.*

God is who gives us the ability to work at peace and holiness. In fact, we cannot do anything without Jesus.

John 15:5 (CJB) *I am the vine and you are the branches. Those who stay united with me, and I with them, are the ones who bear much fruit; because apart from me you can't do a thing.*

Philippians 2:13 (AMP)

For it is [not your strength, but it is] God who is effectively at work in you, both to will and to work [that is, strengthening, energizing, and creating in you the longing and the ability to fulfill your purpose] for His good pleasure.

If the Lord has imputed Jesus's righteousness to those who trust in Him, and if it is the Lord who enables us to live in peace, why are we told to "work at it?" We are His hands and feet on the earth. We trust Jesus to work through us and empower us through His Holy Spirit living in us, but that does not mean that we can just stand there and expect peace to materialize in a relationship. We still need to talk to people and work things out asking the Lord to guide our conversations and even guard our tongues at times.

We must ask ourselves if there is any disunity or disagreement between us and another believer? If so, we need to make it a matter of prayer asking the Lord how best to approach the person and work out peace with them. Then, as much as it depends on us, proceed under the guidance of the Holy Spirit.

Father, sometimes relationships even between brothers and sisters in Christ can be challenging. Help us to treat others the way we would like to be treated (Matthew 7:12). Help us to be quick to listen and slow to an-

ger (James 1:19) Help us to pursue peace by the power of the Holy Spirit.

MAY THE GOD OF PEACE EQUIP YOU

Now may the God of peace^{G1515}, who through the blood
of the eternal covenant brought back from the dead
our Lord Jesus, that great Shepherd of the sheep, equip
you with every good thing to do His will. And may He
accomplish in us what is pleasing in His sight through
Jesus Christ, to whom be glory forever and ever. Amen.

Hebrews 13:20-21

20 God is called "the God of peace" a number of times in the Pauline writings (Ro 15:33; 16:20; 2Co 13:11; Php 4:9; 1Th 5:23). "Peace" connotes the fullest prosperity of the whole man, taking up as it does the OT concept of the Hebrew shalom (see comments on 7:2). Here it reminds us that all our prosperity is centered in God and that a well-rounded life depends on him. The expression is especially suitable in view of what the letter discloses of the condition of the readers. They have had to cope with some form of persecution and were still not free from opposition. They were tempted to leave Christianity and have had to be warned of the dangers of apostasy. They may have had doubts about who their true leaders were. It is well for them to be reminded that real peace is in God. (106)

It is God working in us that enables us to do anything worthwhile for His kingdom. We obey the Lord, submit to His will and purpose, rely on His Holy Spirit who dwells within us for our every need, and please Him by giving Him all the honor and glory. (107)

God is our peace. It is He who takes our broken pieces, our shattered lives, and makes a new creation (2 Corinthians 5:17) with nothing broken, nothing missing, completely whole—peace. Since God was able to raise Christ from the dead, and Jesus is still shepherding His people from the right hand of the Father, the Lord is certainly able to equip us, enable us to do whatever He calls us to do. We are most at peace when we are operating within God's will for us, when we are pleasing to God.

Are you experiencing God's peace? We have the peace of God when we have peace with God by trusting in Jesus's sacrifice on the cross. If you are certain you have trusted Jesus but still feel broken or fragmented or anxious, take everything to Him and ask the God of peace to restore you to wholeness in Him.

Father, when we are feeling anxious or just not quite whole, give us a nudge from the Holy Spirit to lay everything at the foot of the cross and leave it there. Help us to release the tension and relax in the peace You provide.

Worship with Evie singing "Give Them All to Jesus":
https://www.youtube.com/watch?v=DsOnwWsHnIw

WISDOM FROM ABOVE

But the wisdom from above is, first of all, pure, then peaceful[G1516], kind, open to reason, full of mercy and good fruits, without partiality and without hypocrisy. And peacemakers[G1515] who sow seed in peace[G1515] raise a harvest of righteousness.

James 3:17-18

In James 3:13-18, James contrasts the wisdom of the world (13-16) with the wisdom from above (17-18). In studying the passages in this devotional book, we have often seen that being "peaceable"—able to live peacefully with others—is one of the characteristics we as Christ-followers should cultivate. Every trait listed in the Fruit of the Spirit in Galatians 5:22-23 is important, but whether or not we maintain peace in relationships is definitely observable from the outside. We live in a litigious society: people bring lawsuits over things that seem trivial or even ridiculous to others. We may not bring a lawsuit in a matter, but are we quick to get "put out of shape" by something said or done by another person? James points out that this attitude of being quick to "get our feathers ruffled" is not wise. Godly wisdom results in living at peace with others. Charles Swindoll has some good comments about this:

> Peaceable. In contrast to the "bitter jealousy" and "selfish ambition" of the unwise, God-given wisdom produces peaceful relationships. The

265

natural tendency is to be argumentative, quarrelsome, belligerent, quick-tempered. But God's supernatural life within us guards against alienating others. Rather, it seeks to remove ill will. Jesus has a promise for those who are peaceable: "Blessed are the peacemakers, for they shall be called sons of God" (Matt. 5:9). (108)

Read the passage of James 3:13-18, and honestly ask yourself which type of person you are. Do you most resemble the one with "worldly wisdom" or the one with "Godly wisdom?" Only the Holy Spirit can redirect you to operate with "wisdom from above." If this is an area of struggle for you, ask the Lord to help you. According to His word, He will answer that prayer:

James 1:5 (VOICE) *If you don't have all the wisdom needed for this journey, then all you have to do is ask God for it; and God will grant all that you need. He gives lavishly and never scolds you for asking.*

Father, help us not to rely on the world's wisdom even though it may sometimes seem good to our ears or even logical. Help us instead to seek Your wisdom through prayer and Bible study. Help us not to move until we are at peace that we are moving the direction You want us to go.

Listen to Rugged Cross Revival singing "Wisdom from Above": https://www.youtube.com/watch?v=pjUjEJ_a8no&list=RDpjUjEJ_a8no&start_radio=1

Worship along with the song "Freedom From Fear": https://www.youtube.com/watch?v=cNBDpIpQH-Po&list=RDcNBDpIpQHPo&start_radio=1

GRACE AND PEACE BE YOURS IN ABUNDANCE

May grace (spiritual blessing) and peace[G1515] *be given you in increasing abundance – that spiritual peace to be realized in and through Christ, freedom from fears, agitating passions and moral conflicts.*

1 Peter 1:2b (AMP)

> G1515 ĕirēnē—peace (lit. or fig.); by impl. prosperity: - one, peace, quietness, rest, + set at one again. (109)

Like Paul, Peter used "Grace and Peace" as an opening to his letters. It's hard to imagine beginning Sunday school by saying, "Good morning, y'all. Grace and peace be yours in abundance." I think everyone would look at us pretty strangely. It's even a more remote idea to walk up to a Christian friend at work or in the neighborhood and greet them in this manner. But what a wonderful greeting it is! We love the Amplified Version above. Are these the things we hope for our fellow believers? People are torn in so many directions in our lightning paced society. We sometimes feel fragmented and agitated. The peace Peter asked the Lord to give his brothers in Christ was a peace that would restore them to wholeness and oneness with God. We desire this peace for ourselves and pray that you may have it as well.

Perhaps if we greet or leave each other with this blessing as Peter did, we can start a movement in the direction of relying on God's grace for our well-being. When we realize the power that we have in Christ to live abundantly as God intended, rather than just exist from day to day, the world might just be turned upside down again!

Acts 17:6 *But when they could not find them, they dragged Jason and some other brothers before the city officials, shouting, "These men who have turned the world upside down have now come here . . ."*

Father, help us to bless others not just with words but with loving actions, giving of ourselves as Christ gave Himself for us.

SEEK PEACE AND PURSUE IT

Finally, all of you, be like-minded and sympathetic, love as brothers, be tenderhearted and humble. Do not repay evil with evil or insult with insult, but with blessing, because to this you were called so that you may inherit a blessing. For, "Whoever would love life and see good days must keep his tongue from evil and his lips from deceitful speech. He must turn from evil and do good; he must seek peace^{G1515} and pursue^{G1377} it.

1 Peter 3:8-11

This passage brought to mind a verse from one of Paul's letters:

Romans 12:21 (VOICE) *Never let evil get the best of you; instead, overpower evil with the good.*

Paul was rephrasing what Jesus taught in the Sermon on the Mount:

Matthew 5:44 (KJV) *But I say unto you, Love your enemies, bless them that curse you, do good to them that hate you, and pray for them which despitefully use you, and persecute you . . .*

When we show love to our enemies, bless them, and pray for them, we may even turn enemies into friends. Keeping our tongues from evil and deceitful speech is a hard thing:

James 3:8 (VOICE) *But no man has ever demonstrated the ability to tame his own tongue! It is a spring of restless evil, brimming with toxic poisons.*

The only one who ever tamed His tongue successfully was Jesus the God-Man, and He is the only one who can tame our tongues. The Holy Spirit can help us to "bridle" our tongues if we can only pause before reacting and ask the Lord to help us respond correctly. Holding our tongue when our flesh causes us to want to lash out at someone is an essential component of pursuing peace. We don't just hope we can make peace with someone, we have to diligently run after peace:

> G1377 To follow or press hard after, to pursue with earnestness and diligence in order to obtain, to go after with the desire of obtaining (Rom. 9:30, 31; 12:13; 14:19; 1 Cor. 14:1; Phil. 3:12, 14; 1 Thess. 5:15; 1 Tim. 6:11; 2 Tim. 2:22; Heb. 12:14; 1 Pet. 3:11) (110)

> 3:10 love life and see good days. Peter employed apt scriptural confirmation of his exhortation in v. 9, by quoting from Ps. 34:12–16. The believer has been granted the legacy to enjoy his life (John 10:10). In this section, Peter gave straightforward advice on how to experience that rich joy and fullness of life, even in the midst of a hostile environment. The requirements of the fulfilled life include a humble, loving attitude to-

ward everyone (v. 8), a nonvindictive response toward revilers (v. 9), pure and honest speech (v. 10), a disdain for sin and pursuit of peace (v. 11), and a right motive, i.e., to work the righteousness that pleases the omniscient Lord (v. 12; cf. Matt. 5:38–48; Rom. 12:14, 17; 1 Cor. 4:12; 5:11; 1 Thess. 5:15).

Psalm 34:12-14 (ESV) *What man is there who desires life and loves many days, that he may see good? Keep your tongue from evil and your lips from speaking deceit. Turn away from evil and do good; seek peace and pursue it.*

How tame is your tongue? We both confess that ours are not as tame as we would like them to be. How can we improve? We must seek peace and diligently hunt it down. We must ask the Lord to put a guard on our tongues and slow us down before we speak harshly or deceitfully. Living at peace with others is not always easy. In fact, sometimes it is downright hard. This really starts in our thoughts. If we dwell on how someone wronged us, we are apt to let those thoughts tumble out as words. Once those words are let loose, we cannot put them back in. This was illustrated in chapel time at Glenview Christian School as when the toothpaste is squeezed out of the tube, you cannot put it back in!

Father, only You can enable us to tame our tongues, to think before speaking, and return kindness when some-

one has unleashed evil against us in words or actions. Give us the strength needed to overcome evil with good.

"FAMILYSHIP"

Greet one another with a kiss of love. Peace^{G1515} to all of you who are in Christ.

1 Peter 5:14

Peter ends this remarkable letter of hope by re-emphasizing love and peace. Believers were to greet one another with a "kiss of love" (5:14). This formal kiss was a sign of peace among early Christians, demonstrating their brotherly affection, commitment, and unity (1 Cor. 16:20). The outward kiss reflected the inward peace between believers. This is why he can write, "Peace be to you all who are in Christ." (112)

The "holy kiss" was an outward sign of unity, peace, and commitment to one another as brothers and sisters in Christ just as baptism is the outward sign of our surrender and submission to Jesus reflecting the change in our hearts. The holy kiss was usually between two men or two women, not for members of the opposite sex. Sadly, today, two people of the same sex kissing, even on the cheek, probably would be accused of being homosexual. The holy kiss in the culture of the early church would correspond to our shaking hands or a friendly hug. It indicated that they considered each other to be family. Peter left them a blessing of peace because in Christ we have peace with God and peace within, and we should be at peace with each other.

Do relationships in your church or small group resemble a loving family circle, or are they closer to a family feud? When we are in Christ, as we have seen, we need to work at unity among believers. When peace between Christ-followers is disrupted, we need to make every effort to restore it. Susan has a word for the closeness we feel with other Christians. It is "familyship" because it is not limited to fellows, LOL. Are you enjoying peaceful "familyship" within your local body of believers? If not, is there something you can do to restore peace?

Father, we thank You for the "familyship" we enjoy not only with our local church but with members of Your family throughout the world. Let our love for each other be evident to those who are not yet a part of Your family and be used by You to draw them into a saving relationship with Jesus.

Anyone who has trusted Jesus's atoning blood spilled on the cross is now a brother or sister in the family of God. Worship with the News Boys singing "Family of God": https://www.youtube.com/watch?v=V6kOkIJV-oM

MULTIPLICATION, NOT ADDITION

Grace and peace[G1515] be multiplied to you through the knowledge of God and of Jesus our Lord.

2 Peter 2:1

1:2 The apostle's lofty prayer for his readers is that grace and peace might be multiplied to them in the knowledge of God and of Jesus our Lord. He wants them to have this knowledge by the sustaining, empowering grace of God in their everyday lives. He wants their hearts to be guarded by the peace of God that passes all understanding. But this is not to be given in small doses! He desires these blessings to be multiplied in volume, not added in small segments. How can these blessings be multiplied? It is in the knowledge of God and of Jesus our Lord. The better we know God, the more we experience grace and peace. We do better by dwelling in the secret place of the Most High than by making occasional visits there. Those who live in the sanctuary rather than in the suburbs find the secret of God's grace and peace. (113)

Peter doesn't hope for just a little added grace and peace but hopes to see those blessings multiplied in their lives! Multiplication increases something much faster than addition. I think most of us would like our peace to be multiplied, increased exponentially; we do not want Jesus to give us a slightly larger portion but to heap it on! (Like Susan puts whipped cream on chocolate pie. LOL) Yes, God is the one who grants us grace and peace, and we certainly need to ask Him to increase those blessings. However, Peter shows us how to see grace and peace grow in our lives: we need to increase our knowledge of Christ by spending time in the Word and in prayer. Paul saw our need for this deepening of our knowledge as well:

Philippians 3:10 (AMPC) *[For my determined purpose is] that I may know Him [that I may progressively become more deeply and intimately acquainted with Him, perceiving and recognizing and understanding the wonders of His Person more strongly and more clearly], and that I may in that same way come to know the power outflowing from His resurrection [which it exerts over believers], and that I may so share His sufferings as to be continually transformed [in spirit into His likeness even] to His death . . .*

When we make a new friend, we barely know them. However, if we continue spending time with that person, we will get to know them on a deeper level; and they will know us better as well. The way we develop friendships that feel like family members, the type of friendships wherein we finish each other's sentences, is to spend more and more time with the person. We need to ask ourselves how deeply we know Jesus. The only way to know more of Him is to spend time with Him through Bible study, meditating on Scripture, and praying. How much time have we invested in getting to know our Lord? The more time we spend with Jesus, the more grace and peace we will experience.

Father, we desire more of Your blessings. Help us to invest more time in knowing Jesus intimately rather than just a surface relationship. We do not want to be casual acquaintances. We want the presence of Your grace and peace working in and through us in super abundance.

Listen to "Grace and Peace a Song of Unending Love":https://www.youtube.com/watch?v=nZeXi-UbQHEM&list=RDnZeXiUbQHEM&start_radio=1

BE FOUND AT PEACE BECAUSE JESUS HOLDS THE FUTURE

Therefore, beloved, as you anticipate these things, make every effort to be found at peace[G1515]*—spotless and blameless in His sight.*

2 Peter 3:14

The context of this verse is that Peter has been talking about the "day of the Lord" when Jesus will come as righteous Judge. The heavens and the earth will be destroyed by fire, but those who have trusted in Jesus will look forward to a new Heaven and a new earth. Since we are covered by the blood of Christ, the final Passover Lamb, we do not need to fear that day. We are protected much like the children of Israel were saved from the death of the firstborn because they were covered by the blood of the lamb on their door posts and lintels.

Exodus 12:23 (NASB) *For the Lord will pass through to strike the Egyptians; but when He sees the blood on the lintel and on the two doorposts, the Lord will pass over the door and will not allow the destroyer to come into your houses to strike you.*

We will enjoy the peace of Christ because we are secure in our relationship with Him as John MacArthur explains:

3:14 in peace. When Christ returns, each Christian should be found enjoying the peace of Christ which knows no worry or fear about the day of the Lord or the judgment of Christ (cf. Phil. 4:6, 7). To have this peace means that the Christian has a strong sense of assurance of his salvation and a life of obedience to Christ (cf. 1 John 4:17). without spot and blameless. Christians should have a spotless character and a blameless reputation. These characteristics are in graphic contrast to the false teachers (cf. 2:13), but like Christ (1 Pet. 1:19). (114)

1 John 4:17 *And as we live in God, our love grows more perfect. So we will not be afraid on the day of judgment, but we can face him with confidence because we live like Jesus here in this world.*

Because we belong to Jesus, we need not fear the day of judgment. His Holy Spirit works in us to become more and more like Him. By His power, we are salt and light in this world, bringing glory to God (Matthew 5:13-14). The good deeds we do, the Christ-like character traits—Fruit of the Spirit—that we exhibit are evidence that we have been saved by His grace and transformed by His Spirit within us.

Do you fear the "end times"? Are you nervous about being judged at the day of the Lord? If you are confident that you have trusted in Jesus, there is no need for fear.

The full name of the book of Revelation is "The Revelation of Jesus Christ." So much is preached about the Antichrist and all the judgements, but our focus should be on the Conquering King, our Lord, Jesus Christ. Be confident that no matter what comes in the future, you are securely held by Jesus (John 10:27-30).

Father, we do not know everything about the future. We cannot even predict what will happen this afternoon! Thank You that we can be confident that no matter what happens—prosperity or persecution, life or death—we belong to You, and we do not walk through this life alone. We are confident that when our earthly existence ceases, we will immediately be with You!

Worship with the Isaacs singing "I Know Who Holds Tomorrow:"
https://www.youtube.com/watch?v=9K9LPY9A1uI

GREETING OF GRACE, MERCY, AND PEACE

Grace, mercy, and peace, which come from God the Father and from Jesus Christ—the Son of the Father—will continue to be with us who live in truth and love.

2 John 1:3 (NLT)

Notice that in 1:3, John inseparably links "truth and love" to the grace, mercy, and peace that come from God the Father and God the Son. Firm conviction in a saving knowledge of the truth should always be accompanied by love, just as unconditional love for others should be extended within the bounds of doctrinal truth. How these two should be kept in balance requires discernment. Commentator John R. W. Stott puts it well: "Our love grows soft if it is not strengthened by truth, and our truth grows hard if it is not softened by love." (115)

Verse 3 At the time John's letters were written, the salutation of a letter ended with a greeting. Most of the NT letters follow this custom but give it a special Christian character, such as "grace and peace to you" (Ro 1:7; cf. 1Pe 1:2) or "grace, mercy and peace from God the Father and Christ Jesus our Lord" (1Ti 1:2). Here, however, John adds a significant variation to this custom. Rather than wishing or praying that God may grant us peace, he turns it into a promise that God's mercy and grace will be ours if we truly remain in his truth and love. In the next section, "truth" and "love" continue to be the chief topic. (116)

God is the One who gives us grace, mercy, and peace through our trusting in and surrendering to Jesus as His Son. We feel the full measure of those treasured blessings when we continue to live in His truth and love. As we have studied through the Fruit of the Spirit, we have truly found that every one of those traits is only possible because God loves us. Love is the foundational fruit without which we cannot completely cultivate the other eight. However, love isn't just a warm, fuzzy feeling or accepting people right where they are. God's love cares enough about us to convict us of sin, and then when we accept the truth that we cannot possibly live up to God's perfection, shows us the saving grace of Jesus's death on the cross in our place. God's love does not leave us in our sin. He shows it to us, provides the solution in Jesus's sacrifice, then once we trust Jesus, gives us the Holy Spirit to empower us to change anything that falls short of glorifying God. We are not showing love in truth when we allow a person to remain stuck in a cycle of sin. Sometimes, the most loving thing we can do is to confront a person with truth. However, the command to "speak the truth in love" is not just about what we say but how we say it:

Ephesians 4:15 (AMPC) *Rather, let our lives lovingly express truth [in all things, speaking truly, dealing truly, living truly]. Enfolded in love, let us grow up in every way and in all things into Him Who is the Head, [even] Christ (the Messiah, the Anointed One).*

The key to remaining in a state of peace, is to continue growing in God's love and truth. As we grow in our knowledge of Jesus—who He is, how He lived, what He taught—and live out what He has shown us in truth and love, we will experience overflowing grace, mercy, and peace.

Do you want to experience true peace? Grow in God's truth and love. Spend more time in His word, in prayer, and in "familyship" with other Christ-followers. When the Holy Spirit brings conviction, respond by confessing and turning away from the sin—anything that separates us from the goodness of God and God Himself—that He has shown you. God's promise is that He will forgive you and cleanse you. It is truly a peaceful feeling to know you can stand before the Lord completely clean.

1 John 1:9 (VOICE) *But if we own up to our sins, God shows that He is faithful and just by forgiving us of our sins and purifying us from the pollution of all the bad things we have done.*

Father, thank You for extending grace to us when we were still sinners. Thank You that forgiveness is available to us when we confess, when we agree with You that we have messed up. Thank You for enabling us to be at peace, completely tranquil and secure, even in the middle of the chaos of stressful situations.

Worship with Adam Crabb singing "Please Forgive Me"
https://www.youtube.com/watch?v=vkyiwMZb6Io
The closed captioning is not the best, but Adam pronounces the words clearly.

MULTIPLIED BLESSINGS

*Jude, a servant of Jesus Christ and a brother of James,
To those who are called, loved by God the Father, and
kept^{G5083} in Jesus Christ: Mercy, peace^{G1515}, and love be
multiplied^{G4129} to you.*

Jude 1:1-2

Jude was the half-brother of Jesus, but instead of
making that claim to fame, he leans wholeheartedly into humility by identifying himself as the bondser-
vant of Jesus. He places himself under the authority of
Jesus as the Christ—the Greek word for Messiah. He
does make the claim that he is the brother of James,
Christ's other half-brother, to give himself credentials
as a teacher as James led the church in Jerusalem. He
addresses his letter to those who have been called by
the Holy Spirit because of God's love and grace and kept
or sustained by Jesus, the Son—all of which describes
true Christians. What is meant by kept? This means Jesus not only saves us but preserves us, keeps us in right
standing with God. In other words, we cannot lose our
salvation because it does not depend on us to keep it. If
we were not able to save ourselves, we are not able to
take away our salvation ourselves. We depend totally on
Jesus, and He promises to hold on tight to us.

G5083 tēréō . . .Figuratively meaning to keep
in safety, preserve, maintain, with the acc. of
thing (Eph. 4:3; 2 Tim. 4:7; Jude 1:6, negative-

ly, deserting their first estate; Sept.: Prov. 16:17). Figuratively, with the acc. and adjuncts: of persons (2 Cor. 11:9; 1 Tim. 5:22; James 1:27); with an adv. (1 Thess. 5:23); with the dat. of person (Jude 1:1). (117)

John 10:27-28 (NASB) *My sheep listen to My voice, and I know them, and they follow Me; and I give them eternal life, and they will never perish; and no one will snatch them out of My hand.*

Since we trust in Jesus who holds us securely, we will abound in grace, mercy, and peace.

G4129. plēthúnō; fut. plēthunṓ, from pléthos (4128), multitude. To make full; hence, to multiply, increase. (I) Trans. (2 Cor. 9:10; Heb. 6:14 quoted from Gen. 22:17 [cf. 3:16]). Pass. plēthúnomai, to be multiplied, increased in number (Acts 6:7; 7:17; 9:31); in magnitude, extent (Matt. 24:12; Acts 12:24; Sept.: Gen. 7:17, 18). Followed by the dat. of person (1 Pet. 1:2, meaning to abound to someone; 2 Pet. 1:2; Jude 1:2). (118)

Are you leading a life that abounds in grace, mercy, and peace—the abundant life Jesus promised to His followers?

John 10:10 (AMP) *The thief comes only in order to steal and kill and destroy. I came that they may have and*
287

enjoy life, and have it in abundance [to the full, till it overflows].

A joy-filled, truly abundant life is yours if you have surrendered your life to Jesus. If you are not experiencing grace, mercy, and peace in increasing amounts, ask the Lord to reveal anything in your life that needs to change. Then by the power of the Holy Spirit in you make that change. Do not let the enemy steal your joy! Call on the name of the Lord to strengthen you.

Father, You only give us good and perfect gifts. If we are stubbornly putting up any roadblock in the way of having grace, mercy, and peace, please tear those roadblocks down. Reveal our sin to us so we can confess it and be made clean again. Restore us to keep Satan from stealing our joy.

Worship with Jason Crabb singing "Good Morning, Mercy": https://www.youtube.com/watch?v=aRb-9C4v8XtA

PEACE WITH GOD, THE PEACE OF GOD, AND PEACE WITH OTHERS

Peace with God has been purchased
through Jesus's death on the cross
and is offered to us freely
because Jesus paid the cost.

The righteous wrath of God
demanded death as our penalty.
But Jesus was the spotless Lamb
who took the place of you and me.

We did not and cannot earn God's love.
He chose to offer us grace
by sending His Son to live as a man
then be crucified in our place.

In order to live at peace with God,
we to need to place our total trust
in the fact that Jesus died and rose,
and He did it for each of us.

Once we accept the gracious gift
of peace with God through Christ,
we have access to the peace of God

each and every day of our lives.
We need not suffer anxiety
because we can cast every care
on Jesus who saves and keeps us;
just take it to Him in prayer.

We live in complete confidence
that we are secure in God's hands,
and we need not fret nor worry
because we can trust in His plans.

Once we have peace with the Father
by trusting in Jesus the Son
and live daily in the peace of His presence,
then peace with others can be won.

We need to strive for peace with others
as much as it depends upon us.
Especially with our sisters and brothers,
we should live in unity and not constant fuss.

We've studied many Bible verses,
instructions on how to foster peace.
We need to practice all we have learned
to ensure that strivings cease.

Peace with people is only possible
when peace with God and peace within are found.
Then this fruit of the Spirit
can be cultivated and even abound!

FACETS OF PEACE

PEACE WITH GOD

God Grants Abram Peace
The Blessing of Obedience is Peace
Sar Shalom: Prince of Peace
Everlasting Kingdom of Peace
Beautiful Feet
Suffering Servant Brings Shalom
Go in Peace, and be Free
Prophet to Prepare the Way for the Prince of Peace
Peace on Earth
Faith Leads to Peace
Parade of the Prince of Peace
If Only You had Known
Peace be with You
Peter Proclaims Gospel of Peace to the Gentiles
Grace and Peace to Believers in Rome
The Peace of God is Inclusive, Not Exclusive
Through God's Grace, I Stand in Peace
Filled with Joy and Peace
Fruit of the Spirit: Peace
I Will Testify About His Blood
Jesus: The Source of Peace for All Who Trust Him
Boots of Peace?
Prevailing Peace
The Son Bled Peace into the World
God of Peace Himself Sanctifies Us
"Familyship"

Peace with God, the Peace of God, and Peace with Others

PEACE OF GOD

God Grants Abram Peace
Jacob Promises Tithe to God and Peace
Go in Peace to Egypt
The Blessing of Obedience is Peace
Peace is a Present from God
Peace Through Submission to God's Plans
Peaceful Sleep
Blessed with Strength and Peace
Peace Prevails for the Meek Who Seek God's Kingdom
Peace Will Proliferate
The Lord Will Speak Peace
Great Peace
In Favor of Peace
Pray for the Peace of Jerusalem
Keeping Commandments Provides Peace
Peaceful Paths of Wisdom
Peace-filled Joy
Sar Shalom: Prince of Peace
Everlasting Kingdom of Peace
Kept in Perfect Peace
Led Forth in Peace
Peace, Be Still
Go in Peace, and be Free
Prophet to Prepare the Way for the Prince of Peace
Peace on Earth

Christmas Poem by a Soldier's Mom
Shalom for Simeon
Faith Leads to Peace
Parade of the Prince of Peace
Peace be with You
Legacy of Peace
Peace During Tribulation
Sent Out with Peace
Peace for the Doubter
Respite to Refuel and Refine
Grace and Peace to Believers in Rome
The Peace of God is Inclusive, Not Exclusive
The Mind of The Spirit is Life and Peace
God of Peace
Trending Now: Grace and Peace
Fruit of the Spirit: Peace
Boots of Peace?
Prevailing Peace
Focus on Precious Perceptions
Grace and Peace as a Greeting
Let God's Peace Reign and be Thankful!
May Your Peace Reign
Peace Always in All Ways
Grace, Mercy, and Peace
Grace and Peace to Philemon
Discipline Yields the Peaceful Fruit of Righteousness
May the God of Peace Equip You
Grace and Peace be Yours in Abundance
"Familyship"
Multiplication, Not Addition

Be Found at Peace Because Jesus Holds the Future
Greeting of Grace, Mercy, and Peace
Multiplied Blessings
Peace with God, the Peace of God, and Peace with Others
Our Father's Joy, Approval, and Peace

PEACE WITH OTHERS

Covenant of Peace Between Isaac and Abimelech
Jealousy Disrupts Peace
Go in Peace to Egypt
Advice to Keep the Peace
Peace Pact Between Saul's Son and the Anointed One
Passionately Pursue Peace
Peace Will Proliferate
In Favor Peace
Enemies Live at Peace with Us
Peacemakers Look Like Papa
Peace Preservers
Overcome Evil with Good
Pursue What Promotes Peace
Filled with Joy and Peace
God of Peace to Crush Satan
Perfect Harmony: Live in Peace
Fruit of the Spirit: Peace
Jesus: The Source of Peace for All Who Trust Him
Practice and Preserve the Bond of Peace
Boots of Peace?
Peace Progresses from God's Love

Live in Peace with Leaders
Hunt Down Harmony
Grace and Peace to Philemon
Pursue Peace
Wisdom from Above
Seek Peace and Pursue It
"Familyship"
Peace with God, the Peace of God, and Peace with Others

JEWELS OF SALVATION

❖ *Romans 3:22-24 And this righteousness from God comes through faith in Jesus Christ to all who believe. There is no distinction,* **for all have sinned and fall short of the glory of God** *and are justified freely by His grace through the redemption that is in Christ Jesus.*

Everyone on earth has sinned. Sin is both doing things that go against what God tells us to do in the Bible and failing to do the good things He instructs us to do. This failure brings the wrath of God on us, and Jesus is the **only way** to make peace with God. John 14:6 "Jesus answered, 'I am the way and the truth and the life. No one comes to the Father except through Me.'"

❖ *Romans 6:20-23 For when you were slaves to sin, you were free of obligation to righteousness. What fruit did you reap at that time from the things of which you are now ashamed? The outcome of those things is death. But now that you have been set free from sin and have become slaves to God, the fruit you reap leads to holiness, and the outcome is eternal life.* **For the wages of sin is death, but the gift of God is eternal life in Christ Jesus our Lord.**

The punishment for sin is death. The official term

is "substitutionary atonement" which simply means you were sentenced to the death penalty, but Jesus volunteered to die on the cross in your place in order for you to be set free. Jesus died a painful death to redeem you from slavery to sin and spare you from the wrath of the righteous, Holy God.

❖ *Romans 5:6-8 For at just the right time, while we were still powerless, Christ died for the ungodly. Very rarely will anyone die for a righteous man, though for a good man someone might possibly dare to die.* **But God proves His love for us in this: While we were still sinners, Christ died for us.**

Jesus died while we were still sinners. "For God so loved the world that **He gave His one and only Son**, that everyone who believes in Him shall not perish but have eternal life." John 3:16.

❖ *Romans 10:8-10 But what does it say? "The word is near you; it is in your mouth and in your heart," that is, the word of faith we are proclaiming: that* ***if you confess with your mouth, "Jesus is Lord," and believe in your heart that God raised Him from the dead, you will be saved.*** *For with your heart you believe and are justified, and with your mouth you confess and are saved.*

1 Corinthians 15:3-4 "For what I received I passed

on to you as of first importance: that Christ died for our sins according to the Scriptures, that He was buried, that He was raised on the third day according to the Scriptures . . ." If you believe that Jesus is the Son of God who died for you and was raised to life, then trust in—rely on—Him to save you from the wrath of God, you can belong to Jesus.

❖ *Romans 10:11-13 It is just as the Scripture says: "Anyone who believes in Him will never be put to shame." For there is no difference between Jew and Greek: The same Lord is Lord of all, and gives richly to all who call on Him, for,* **"Everyone who calls on the name of the Lord will be saved."**

How do you become a member of the family of God? Pray—talk to God admitting that you cannot be good enough because you could *never* perfectly obey all His commands. Tell Him you trust that Jesus died on the cross to save you from slavery to sin and the wrath of God. Ask God to place His Holy Spirit in you and change you from the inside out. Thank Him for giving you life in His presence forever.

BELIEVER'S BENEFITS

The obvious benefit of trusting in Jesus, the Son of God who died for you and was raised from the grave to return to the right hand of His Father, and surrendering your life to him, is that instead of spending eternity separated from God and all that is good you will live in His presence in complete peace and joy. However, those who become the Lord's children by relying on Jesus gain many other things in this current life on earth. Here are a few:

❖   Lord, we thank you for freeing us from slavery to sin and providing a way to flee temptation! Romans 6:6 "We know that our old self was crucified with Him so that the body of sin might be rendered powerless, that we should no longer be slaves to sin." This does not mean that a believer will never sin again. It means he/she now has a choice to tap into the Holy Spirit's power to resist the urge to give in to temptation. "No temptation has seized you except what is common to man. And God is faithful; He will not let you be tempted beyond what you can bear. But when you are tempted, He will also provide an escape, so that you can stand up under it" (1 Corinthians 10:13).

❖   Lord, thank You that nothing can separate us from Your love! "For I am convinced that neither death nor life, neither angels nor principalities, neither the present nor the future, nor any powers, neither height nor depth, nor anything else in all creation, will be able to separate us from the love of God that is in Christ Jesus our Lord" (Romans 8:38-39).

❖   Lord, thank You that our salvation is secure and cannot be lost! John 10:27-29 "My sheep listen to My voice; I know them, and they follow Me. I give them eternal life, and they will never perish. No one can snatch them out of My hand. My Father who has given them to Me is greater than all. No one can snatch them out of My Father's hand."

❖   Lord thank you for empowering us to do whatever You call us to do! Philippians 4:13 (AMP) "I can do all things [which He has called me to do] through Him who strengthens and empowers me [to fulfill His purpose—I am self-sufficient in Christ's sufficiency; I am ready for anything and equal to anything through Him who infuses me with inner strength and confident peace.]

❖   Lord, thank You for giving us brothers and sisters all over the world! "Respect everyone, and love the family of believers." 1 Peter 2:17a (NLT).

DICTIONARY OF "SUSANISMS"

Bed-found – This is preferred over "bed-bound" because Susan is not chained to her bed, but these days it is usually where Susan is found.

CareGIVER – Caregivers take care of people. Caretakers maintain houses, buildings, or cemeteries! Susie is my caregiver, and I am hers!

Fam<u>bly</u> – Family by the blood of Jesus.

Familyship – The family of God. We prefer "familyship" over "fellowship" because, obviously, we are not all fellows.

Framily – Friends who have become family because of our mutual love for Jesus, our brothers and sisters in Christ which may include our biological family as well.

Full-weight - Susan is not "dead weight" when we lift her because she is very much alive! We are simply bearing her full weight because she cannot assist us.

Remnants – Susan does not call her shortened legs "stumps," because stumps are something you put in a woodchipper. Her legs are "remnants" because Jesus saves and returns for the remnant.

Tater – This is Susan's nickname or job description for Susie. It is short for facilitator because Susie facilitates many things for her.

Finally, PLEASE do **not** refer to Susan as an invalid. She is not IN-valid. Here is her description of herself:

I AM UNIQUELY FIT FOR HIS SERVICE: A DIVINELY DESIGNED PRESENTATION!

INDEX OF SCRIPTURE REFERENCES

Genesis 3:15	193
Genesis 15:13-21	33
Genesis 26:26-31	36
Genesis 28:20-22	39
Genesis 37:3-4	42
Exodus 4:18	45
Exodus 12:23	277
Exodus 18:23	47
Leviticus 26:3-9	49
Numbers 6:22-27	52
Numbers 6:25-26	54
Numbers 24:9	83
Deuteronomy 10:17	162
Judges 6:22-24	56
1 Samuel 15:26-28	59
1 Samuel 18:1	60
1 Samuel 20:42	59
2 Chronicles 19:7	162
Psalm 4:8	62
Psalm 23:1	65
Psalm 29:11	64
Psalm 34:12-14	270
Psalm 34:13-15	66
Psalm 37:11, 37-38	68
Psalm 72:7	70
Psalm 85:8-9	73
Psalm 119:9-11	86, 131
Psalm 119:105	131

Psalm 119:165	76
Psalm 120:5-7	79
Psalm 122:6-8	82
Psalm 133:1	43
Psalm 138:3	221
Proverbs 3:1-6	85
Proverbs 3:13-18	89
Proverbs 9:10	89
Proverbs 12:20	90
Proverbs 16:7	92
Proverbs 21:1	72
Isaiah 9:6	95
Isaiah 9:7	98
Isaiah 25:9	130
Isaiah 26:3	40, 96
Isaiah 26:3-4	101
Isaiah 40:3	122
Isaiah 52:7	103
Isaiah 53:4-6	106
Isaiah 55:12	108
Isaiah 57:19	206
Isaiah 61:10	99
Jeremiah 1:4-5	241
Zechariah 13:7	149
Malachi 3:1	122
Malachi 4:2	117, 123
Matthew 5:9	111
Matthew 5:44	268
Matthew 6:9b-10	83
Matthew 20:28	160

Matthew 26:31	150
Matthew 28:18-20	164
Mark 4:39	113
Mark 5:33-34	116
Mark 9:50	120
Mark 14:27	150
Luke 1:76-79	122
Luke 2:13-14	125
Luke 2:14	128
Luke 2:29-32	130
Luke 7:41-42	135
Luke 7:43	135
Luke 7:47	135
Luke 7:50	134
Luke 8:44	116
Luke 19:36-38	138
Luke 19:41-44	141
Luke 19:44b	142
Luke 24:35-43	144
John 1:5	123
John 6:44	240
John 8:12	131
John 9:5	131
John 10:10	88, 232, 285
John 10:11a	65
John 10:27-28	285
John 14:13-14	190
John 14:17	109
John 14:27	147
John 15:5	93, 257

John 16:32-33	149
John 16:33	174
John 20:19-21	153
John 20:22	154
John 20:26-29	156
Acts 9:31	159
Acts 10:27-28	163
Acts 10:34-36	162
Acts 17:6	267
Romans 1:7	166
Romans 2:9-11	169
Romans 5:1-5	174
Romans 8:5-10	177
Romans 8:6	178
Romans 8:10	179
Romans 8:28-30	240
Romans 10:15	103
Romans 12:17-19	80
Romans 12:17-21	180
Romans 12:18	180, 257
Romans 12:21	268
Romans 14:17-19	183
Romans 15:13	187
Romans 15:33	190
Romans 16:20	193
1 Corinthians 1:3	196
2 Corinthians 1:2	196
2 Corinthians 4:16-18	118
2 Corinthians 6:2	142
2 Corinthians 13:11	198

2 Corinthians 13:11	199
Galatians 1:3	196
Galatians 3:28	170
Galatians 5:22-23	201
Ephesians 1:2	196
Ephesians 2:8-9	170
Ephesians 2:11-18	205
Ephesians 2:13	203
Ephesians 2:17	206
Ephesians 4:1-3	210
Ephesians 4:15	282
Ephesians 5:25-27	100
Ephesians 6:15	103
Ephesians 6:13-18	214
Ephesians 6:23-24	217
Philippians 1:2	196
Philippians 1:6	241
Philippians 2:13	258
Philippians 3:2-3	74
Philippians 3:9b	99
Philippians 3:10	275
Philippians 3:20-21	99
Philippians 4:6-7	90, 109, 244
Philippians 4:6-7	221
Philippians 4:8	97
Philippians 4:8-9	223
Colossians 1:1-2	226
Colossians 1:15-20	229
Colossians 1:15-23	230
Colossians 3:14	186

Colossians 3:15-17	233, 235
1 Thessalonians 1:1-2	196
1 Thessalonians 5:12-13	236
1 Thessalonians 5:17	132
1 Thessalonians 5:23-24	239
2 Thessalonians 1:2	196
2 Thessalonians 3:16	243
1 Timothy 1:2	246
1 Timothy 2:1-4	72
1 Timothy 4:12	247
1 Timothy 6:6	58
2 Timothy 1:1-2	246
2 Timothy 2:22	249
2 Timothy 3:12	93
Titus 1:4	196
Philemon 1:1-3	251
Hebrews 7:27	157
Hebrews 12:2	40
Hebrews 12:9-11	254
Hebrews 12:14	257
Hebrews 13:20-21	260
James 1:5	191, 264
James 1:17	191
James 3:1	237
James 3:8	269
James 3:17-18	263
1 Peter 1:2b	266
1 Peter 3:8-11	268
1 Peter 3:3-4	87
1 Peter 5:7	65, 244

1 Peter 5:14 272
2 Peter 2:1 274
2 Peter 3:14 277
1 John 1:9 282
1 John 4:17 278
1 John 5:14 191
2 John 1:3 280
Jude 1:1-2 284

NOTES

1.   Warren Baker and Eugene E. Carpenter, The Complete Word Study Dictionary: Old Testament (Chattanooga, TN: AMG Publishers, 2003), 1145.

2.   Spiros Zodhiates, The Complete Word Study Dictionary: New Testament (Chattanooga, TN: AMG Publishers, 2000).

3.   Strong, James, The New Strong's Exhaustive Concordance of the Bible, (Thomas Nelson, 2009).

4.   Barker, Kenneth L. and Kohlenberger, John R., III, The Expositor's Bible Commentary - Abridged Edition: New Testament, (Zondervan Academic / 2017 / Epub).

5.   Wiersbe, Warren, NKJV Wiersbe Study Bible, (Thomas Nelson, 2021).

6.   Keener, Craig & Walton, John, NIV Cultural Backgrounds Study Bible, (Zondervan, 2016).

7.   MacArthur, John, NKJV MacArthur Study Bible, 2nd Edition, (Thomas Nelson, 1997, 2006, 2019), as quoted on www.biblegateway.com

8.   MacArthur, John, NKJV MacArthur Study Bible, 2nd Edition, (Thomas Nelson, 1997, 2006, 2019), as quoted on www.biblegateway.com

9.   Barker, Kenneth L. and Kohlenberger, John R., III, The Expositor's Bible Commentary - Abridged Edition: New Testament, (Zondervan Academic / 2017 / Epub).

10.   Wiersbe, Warren, NKJV Wiersbe Study Bible, (Thomas Nelson, 2021).

11.   Keener, Craig & Walton, John, NIV Cultural Backgrounds Study Bible, (Zondervan, 2016).

12.   Strong, James, The New Strong's Exhaustive Concordance of the Bible, (Thomas Nelson, 2009).

13.   Evans, Tony, Tony Evans Study Bible, (Holman Bible Publishers, 2017).

14.   Wiersbe, Warren, NKJV Wiersbe Study Bible, (Thomas Nelson, 2021).

15.   Webster, Noah, The American Dictionary of the English Language, 1828 as found at https://webstersdictionary1828.com/

16.   MacDonald, William, Believer's Bible Commentary, (Thomas Nelson, 2016).

17.   Stanley, Charles, NASB Charles F. Stanley Life Principles Bible, (Thomas Nelson, 2020).

18.   Mcgee, J. Vernon, Thru the Bible Commentary Series, (Thomas Nelson, 1988).

19.   Strong, James, The New Strong's Exhaustive Concordance of the Bible, (Thomas Nelson, 2009).

20.   Strong, James, The New Strong's Exhaustive Concordance of the Bible, (Thomas Nelson, 2009).

21.   NKJV Macarthur Study Bible, 2nd Edition, Copyright © 1997, 2006, 2019 by Thomas Nelson.

22.   MacDonald, William, Believer's Bible Commentary, (Thomas Nelson, 2016).

23.   Warren Baker and Eugene E. Carpenter, The Complete Word Study Dictionary: Old Testament (Chattanooga, TN: AMG Publishers, 2003), 517.

24.   Evans, Tony, Tony Evans Study Bible, (Holman Bible Publishers, 2017)

25.   Wiersbe, Warren, NKJV Wiersbe Study Bible Copyright © 2021 by Thomas Nelson.

26.   https://www.gotquestions.org/support-Israel.html

27.   Wiersbe, Warren, NKJV Wiersbe Study Bible, Copyright © 2021 by Thomas Nelson

28.	Warren Baker and Eugene E. Carpenter, The Complete Word Study Dictionary: Old Testament (Chattanooga, TN: AMG Publishers, 2003), 1152.7999

29.	Sproul, R. C., ESV Reformation Study Bible, (Reformation Trust Publishing of Ligonier Ministries, 2021).

30.	Barker, Kenneth L. and Kohlenberger, John R., III, The Expositor's Bible Commentary - Abridged Edition: New Testament, (Zondervan Academic / 2017 / Epub).

31.	Webster, Noah, The American Dictionary of the English Language, 1828. as found at https://webstersdictionary1828.com/

32.	Strong, James, The New Strong's Exhaustive Concordance of the Bible, (Thomas Nelson, 2009).

33.	The ESV Global Study Bible®, ESV Bible® Copyright © 2012 by Crossway. All rights reserved.

34.	Davis, Andrew M., Exalting Jesus in Isaiah (Nashville, TN: Holman Reference, 2017), 314.

35.	Evans, Tony, CSB Tony Evans Study Bible, Copyright © 2017 by Holman Bible Publishers.

36. https://hymnary.org/text/you_shall_go_out_with_joy_and_be_led

37. Strong, James, The New Strong's Exhaustive Concordance of the Bible, (Thomas Nelson, 2009).

38. Charles R. Swindoll, Mark, Swindoll's Living Insights New Testament Commentary (Tyndale House Publishers, 2018), 121.

39. Spiros Zodhiates, The Complete Word Study Dictionary: New Testament (Chattanooga, TN: AMG Publishers, 2000).

40. Spiros Zodhiates, The Complete Word Study Dictionary: New Testament (Chattanooga, TN: AMG Publishers, 2000).

41. NKJV MacArthur Study Bible, 2nd Edition, Copyright © 1997, 2006, 2019 by Thomas Nelson.

42. Wiersbe, Warren, NKJV Wiersbe Study Bible, (Thomas Nelson, 2021).

43. Spiros Zodhiates, The Complete Word Study Dictionary: New Testament (Chattanooga, TN: AMG Publishers, 2000).

44. Spiros Zodhiates, The Complete Word Study Dictionary: New Testament (Chattanooga, TN: AMG Publishers, 2000).

45.   NKJV MacArthur Study Bible, 2nd Edition Copyright © 1997, 2006, 2019 by Thomas Nelson. All rights reserved.

46.   Spiros Zodhiates, The Complete Word Study Dictionary: New Testament (Chattanooga, TN: AMG Publishers, 2000).

47.   Charles R. Swindoll, Luke, vol. 3, Swindoll's Living Insights New Testament Commentary (Carol Stream, IL: Tyndale House Publishers, Inc., 2017), 69.

48.   Saint Basil the Great quoted at: https://www.orthodoxchurchquotes.com/2013/07/10/st-basil-the-great-prayer-is-a-request-for-what-is-good/

49.   You may read the entire article at: https://www.gotquestions.org/Jesus-anointed.html   Another good article on this topic is found at: https://bible.org/seriespage/wordless-worship-unnamed-woman-luke-736-50

50.   Strong, James, The New Strong's Exhaustive Concordance of the Bible, (Thomas Nelson, 2009).

51.   Charles R. Swindoll, John, Swindoll's Living Insights New Testament Commentary (Tyndale House Publishers, 2018), 314.

52.   Charles R. Swindoll, John, Swindoll's Living Insights New Testament Commentary (Tyndale House Publishers, 2018), 315.

53.   Evans, Tony, CSB Tony Evans Study Bible, Copyright © 2017 by Holman Bible Publishers.

54.   Charles R. Swindoll, Swindoll's Living Insights New Testament Commentary (Tyndale House Publishers, 2018), 386.

55.   Wiersbe, Warren, NKJV Wiersbe Study Bible, (Thomas Nelson, 2021).

56.   NKJV MacArthur Study Bible, 2nd Edition Copyright © 1997, 2006, 2019 by Thomas Nelson. All rights reserved.

57.   Charles R. Swindoll, Acts, Swindoll's Living Insights New Testament Commentary (Carol Stream, IL: Tyndale House Publishers, Inc., 2016), 205.

58.   Charles R. Swindoll, Romans, vol. 6, Swindoll's Living Insights New Testament Commentary (Carol Stream, IL: Tyndale House Publishers, 2016), 22.

59.   MacDonald, William, Believer's Bible Commentary Copyright © 1989, 1990, 1992, 1995, 2016.

60.   Spiros Zodhiates, The Complete Word Study Dictionary: New Testament (Chattanooga, TN: AMG Publishers, 2000).

61.   Spiros Zodhiates, The Complete Word Study Dictionary: New Testament (Chattanooga, TN: AMG Publishers, 2000).

62.   McGee, J. Vernon, Thru the Bible Commentary Series, (Thomas Nelson, 1988).

63.   Thayer, Joseph, THAYER'S GREEK LEXICON, Electronic Database. Copyright © 2002, 2003, 2006, 2011 by Biblesoft, Inc. All rights reserved. Used by permission. BibleSoft.com

64.   Charles R. Swindoll, Romans, vol. 6, Swindoll's Living Insights New Testament Commentary (Carol Stream, IL: Tyndale House Publishers, 2016), 295.

65.   Read the entire article at:
     https://www.gotquestions.org/disputable-matters. html

66.   Charles R. Swindoll, Romans, vol. 6, Swindoll's Living Insights New Testament Commentary (Carol Stream, IL: Tyndale House Publishers, 2016), 330.

67.   Spiros Zodhiates, The Complete Word Study Dictionary: New Testament (Chattanooga, TN: AMG Publishers, 2000).

68.   Evans, Tony, CSB Tony Evans Study Bible, Copyright © 2017 by Holman Bible Publishers.

69.   Stanley, Charles F., NASB Charles F. Stanley Life Principles Bible, (Thomas Nelson, 2020).

70.   Spiros Zodhiates, The Complete Word Study Dictionary: New Testament (Chattanooga, TN: AMG Publishers, 2000).

71.   MacArthur, John, NKJV MacArthur Study Bible, 2nd Edition Copyright © 1997, 2006, 2019 by Thomas Nelson. All rights reserved.

72.   MacArthur, John, NKJV MacArthur Study Bible, 2nd Edition, Copyright © 1997, 2006, 2019 by Thomas Nelson. All rights reserved.

73.   MacDonald, William, Believer's Bible Commentary, Copyright © 1989, 1990, 1992, 1995, 2016.

74.   Charles R. Swindoll, Romans, vol. 6, Swindoll's Living Insights New Testament Commentary (Carol Stream, IL: Tyndale House Publishers, 2016), 371–372.

75.   Evans, Tony, CSB Tony Evans Study Bible, Copyright © 2017 by Holman Bible Publishers.

76.   Charles R. Swindoll, 1 & 2 Corinthians, vol. 7, Swindoll's Living Insights New Testament Commentary

(Carol Stream, IL: Tyndale House Publishers, 2017), 485.

77.   https://loveinbible.com/how-many-times-is-peace-mentioned-in-the-bible/

78.   Charles R. Swindoll, Galatians, Ephesians, Swindoll's Living Insights New Testament Commentary (Carol Stream, IL: Tyndale House Publishers, Inc., 2015), 200.

79.   https://www.gotquestions.org/He-Himself-is-our-peace.html

80.   Barker, Kenneth L. and Kohlenberger, John R., III, The Expositor's Bible Commentary - Abridged Edition: New Testament, (Zondervan Academic / 2017 / Epub).

81.   Barker, Kenneth L. and Kohlenberger, John R., III, The Expositor's Bible Commentary - Abridged Edition: New Testament, (Zondervan Academic / 2017 / Epub).

82.   Strong, James, The New Strong's Exhaustive Concordance of the Bible, (Thomas Nelson, 2009).

83.   Webster, Noah, The American Dictionary of the English Language, 1828. as found at https://webstersdictionary1828.com/

84.   Charles R. Swindoll, Galatians, Ephesians, Swindoll's Living Insights New Testament Commentary (Carol Stream, IL: Tyndale House Publishers, Inc., 2015), 310–311.

85.   Charles R. Swindoll, Galatians, Ephesians, Swindoll's Living Insights New Testament Commentary (Carol Stream, IL: Tyndale House Publishers, Inc., 2015), 320.

86.   Barker, Kenneth L. and Kohlenberger, John R., III, The Expositor's Bible Commentary - Abridged Edition: New Testament, (Zondervan Academic / 2017 / Epub).

87.   Spiros Zodhiates, The Complete Word Study Dictionary: New Testament (Chattanooga, TN: AMG Publishers, 2000).

88.   Strong, James, The New Strong's Exhaustive Concordance of the Bible, (Thomas Nelson, 2009).

89.   Strong, James, The New Strong's Exhaustive Concordance of the Bible, (Thomas Nelson, 2009).

90.   Spiros Zodhiates, The Complete Word Study Dictionary: New Testament (Chattanooga, TN: AMG Publishers, 2000).

91.   MacArthur, John, NKJV MacArthur Study Bible, 2nd Edition, Copyright © 1997, 2006, 2019 by Thomas Nelson. All rights reserved.

92.   Read the full article at: https://www.gotquestions.org/He-is-before-all-things.html

93.   Strong, James, The New Strong's Exhaustive Concordance of the Bible, (Thomas Nelson, 2009).

94.   Mohler, R Albert, Jr. NIV Grace and Truth Study Bible, Zondervan 2021.

95.   Wiersbe, Warren, NKJV Wiersbe Study Bible, Copyright © 2021 by Thomas Nelson. All rights reserved.

96.   Spiros Zodhiates, The Complete Word Study Dictionary: New Testament (Chattanooga, TN: AMG Publishers, 2000).

97.   Charles R. Swindoll, Insights on 1 & 2 Thessalonians, vol. 10, Swindoll's Living Insights New Testament Commentary (Carol Stream, IL: Tyndale House Publishers, Inc., 2016), 96.

98.   Evans, Tony, CSB Tony Evans Study Bible, Copyright © 2017 by Holman Bible Publishers.

99.   Stanley, Charles, NASB Charles F. Stanley Life Principles Bible, (Thomas Nelson, 2020).

100.   Carson, D.A., Ed., NIV Biblical Theology Study Bible,
Copyright © 2019 by Zondervan.

101.   Charles R. Swindoll, Philippians, Colossians, Philemon, vol. 9, Swindoll's Living Insights New Testament Commentary (Carol Stream, IL: Tyndale House Publishers, Inc., 2017), 204.

102.   Charles R. Swindoll, Philippians, Colossians, Philemon, vol. 9, Swindoll's Living Insights New Testament Commentary (Carol Stream, IL: Tyndale House Publishers, Inc., 2017), 202.

103.   Wiersbe, Warren, NKJV Wiersbe Study Bible, Copyright © 2021 Thomas Nelson.

104.   Green, Steve and High, Bill, This Beautiful Book, (Zondervan, 2019).

105.   Carson, D.A., ed. NIV Biblical Theology Study Bible, Zondervan, 2018.

106.   Barker, Kenneth L. and Kohlenberger, John R., III, The Expositor's Bible Commentary - Abridged Edition: New Testament, (Zondervan Academic / 2017 / Epub).

107.   Stanley, Charles, NASB Charles F. Stanley Life Principles Bible, (Thomas Nelson, 2020).

108.   Charles R. Swindoll, Insights on James, 1 & 2 Peter, vol. 13, Swindoll's Living Insights New Testament Commentary (Carol Stream, IL: Tyndale House Publishers, 2014), 82.

109.   Strong, James, The New Strong's Exhaustive Concordance of the Bible, (Thomas Nelson, 2009).

110.   Spiros Zodhiates, The Complete Word Study Dictionary: New Testament (Chattanooga, TN: AMG Publishers, 2000).

111.   MacArthur, John, NKJV MacArthur Study Bible, 2nd Edition, (Thomas Nelson, 1997, 2006, 2019), as quoted on www.biblegateway.com

112.   Charles R. Swindoll, Insights on James, 1 & 2 Peter, vol. 13, Swindoll's Living Insights New Testament Commentary (Carol Stream, IL: Tyndale House Publishers, 2014), 276–277.

113.   MacDonald, William, Believer's Bible Commentary, (Thomas Nelson, 2016).

114.   MacArthur, John, NKJV MacArthur Study Bible, 2nd Edition, (Thomas Nelson, 1997, 2006, 2019), as quoted on www.biblegateway.com

115.   Charles R. Swindoll, Insights on 1, 2 & 3 John, Jude, vol.14, Swindoll's Living Insights New Testament Commentary (Carol Stream, IL: Tyndale House Publishers, 2018), 140.

116.   Barker, Kenneth L. and Kohlenberger, John R., III, The Expositor's Bible Commentary - Abridged Edition: New Testament, (Zondervan Academic / 2017 / Epub).

117.   Spiros Zodhiates, The Complete Word Study Dictionary: New Testament (Chattanooga, TN: AMG Publishers, 2000).

118.   Spiros Zodhiates, The Complete Word Study Dictionary: New Testament (Chattanooga, TN: AMG Publishers, 2000).

BIBLIOGRAPHY

Baker, Warren and Carpenter, Eugene, eds., *The Complete Word Study Dictionary: Old Testament*, (Chattanooga, TN: AMG Publishers, 2003).

Barker, Kenneth L. and Kohlenberger, John R., III, *The Expositor's Bible Commentary - Abridged Edition: New Testament*, (Zondervan Academic / 2017 / Epub).

Carson, D.A., ed. *NIV Biblical Theology Study Bible*, Zondervan, 2018.

Davis, Andrew M., *Exalting Jesus in Isaiah* (Nashville, TN: Holman Reference, 2017), 314.

Evans, Tony, *Tony Evans Study Bible*, (Holman Bible Publishers, 2017)

Green, Steve and High, Bill, *This Beautiful Book*, (Zondervan, 2019).

Keener, Craig & Walton, John, *NIV Cultural Backgrounds Study Bible*, (Zondervan, 2016).

MacArthur, John, *NKJV MacArthur Study Bible, 2nd Edition*, (Thomas Nelson, 1997, 2006, 2019), as quoted on www.biblegateway.com

MacDonald, William, *Believer's Bible Commentary*, (Thomas Nelson, 2016).

Mcgee, J. Vernon, *Thru the Bible Commentary Series*, (Thomas Nelson, 1988).

Mohler, R Albert, Jr. *NIV Grace and Truth Study Bible*, Zondervan 2021.

Sproul, R. C., *ESV Reformation Study Bible*, (Reformation Trust Publishing of Ligonier Ministries, 2021).

Stanley, Charles, *NASB Charles F. Stanley Life Principles Bible*, (Thomas Nelson, 2020).

Strong, James, *The New Strong's Exhaustive Concordance of the Bible*, (Thomas Nelson, 2009).

Swindoll, *Charles R., Swindoll's Living Insights New Testament Commentary*, (Carol Stream, Illinois, Tyndale House Publishers, 2020).

Thayer, Joseph, *THAYER'S GREEK LEXICON*, Electronic Database. Copyright © 2002, 2003, 2006, 2011 by Biblesoft, Inc. All rights reserved. Used by permission. BibleSoft.com

Webster, Noah, *The American Dictionary of the English Language*, 1828. as found at https://webstersdictionary1828.com/

Wiersbe, Warren, *NKJV Wiersbe Study Bible*, (Thomas Nelson, 2021).

Zodhiates, Spiros, ed., *The Complete Word Study Dictionary: New Testament* (Chattanooga, TN: AMG Publishers, 2000).

Susan Slade and Susie Hale

www.ingramcontent.com/pod-product-compliance
Lightning Source LLC
Chambersburg PA
CBHW050012090426
42733CB00018B/2641